How to Prosper
in Any Recession

by

Dr. Nasir Siddiki

Titles may be purchased in bulk for educational, business, fund-
raising, or sales promotional use. For information, please email
drnsiddiki@wisdomministries.org.

Unless otherwise indicated, all Scripture quotations are taken from
the *New King James Version (NKJV) Copyright © 1982 by Thomas
Nelson, Inc.* or the King James Version of the Bible.

Scripture quotations marked AMP are taken from *The Amplified Bible,* Copyright © 1954, 1958, 1962, 1964, 1965, 1987 by the
Lockman Foundation. Used by permission. All rights reserved.

Scriptures with words in **bold type** are modified by the author for
emphasis.

Project Manager: Dan Withum, Withum & Company

Project Editor: Joshua D. Lease/Aegis Editing
www.AegisEditing.com

How to Prosper in Any Recession

ISBN 978-0-9666779-3-5

Printed and bound in the United States of America

Dedication

I dedicate this book to all my spiritual sons and daughters and all the mighty men and women of God who will not compromise His Word. It is to those who will not be moved by what they see, are immoveable in their faith and trust in the Lord. He will cause you to become an overcomer, more than a conqueror. In Christ Jesus, you will always triumph. May the pages of this book bring revelation, so that you may endure every adversity, knowing that God is faithful. I trust that you will see through this book, that in times of recession, God's plan is always for major wealth transfers to occur.

Contents

Acknowledgements

No project of this magnitude can come together without the efforts of a team of dedicated individuals. They have helped me take a message that God placed in my heart and put it into written form so that many more people, like you, can be blessed.

Of course, I must acknowledge and express my thanks to my Savior, Lord, and Healer, the Lord Jesus Christ, for entrusting this message to me and giving me the ability to share it around the world. My family deserves special thanks for their support, love, and understanding. My staff, which labors many hours with dedication and perseverance, is appreciated more than they'll ever know.

My thanks go out to Dan Withum who managed the production of this book. And without Joshua Lease of Aegis Editing, Marilyn Price, and Gene Gregg, it would not have looked this good.

Foreword

This erudite, eloquent, and immensely thought-provoking work gets to the heart of the principles of financial success and addresses the deepest contradictions within our culture concerning the subject of money and righteousness.

This is indispensable reading for believers who want to live life above the norm and maximize their resources for the Kingdom. This is a profound, authoritative work that spans the wisdom of the ages yet breaks new ground in its approach to financial wealth and will possibly become a classic in this and the next generation.

Dr. Myles Munroe

BFM International

ITWLA

Nassau, Bahamas

Introduction

This book came together as the result of several messages I have recently shared as I travel to churches all over America. As I was observing the economic troubles in the United States and across the world and thinking about their impact on the Church, the Lord began to speak to me about His Kingdom. He reminded me that His economy is not the same as the world's economy and that His economy operates on much higher laws. As I was meditating on these truths, my spiritual mentor, Brother Kenneth Copeland, brought forth a powerful word from the Lord. This word, which I have included within these pages, confirmed what the Lord had been showing me.

As you read this book, I pray that the revelation of *how you can prosper in any recession* will break forth in your heart and that you will rise up in these turbulent times. We should not be moved by the fear of economic downturns, recessions, a floundering world economy, or the facts that may confront us personally. We are neither of this world, nor its economy. When God's children operate in Kingdom principles, they will always get Kingdom results. Learn these principles and be blessed as you read *How to Prosper in Any Recession*.

Chapter 1
Don't Be Part of the Recession

My friend, I am glad you have picked up this book, for you stand at a crossroads. Down one path, the fear the media spreads can become true. Circumstances will mirror the dire predictions they are making.

Down the other, however, you will see something entirely different. Down this path, you listen to another voice—the voice of God. It is in listening to this voice, obeying it, and sowing the seed He tells you that will cause you to receive an extravagant harvest during a recession.

In fact, there are three harvests coming to our land, and this is why I am going to talk to you about prospering in *any* recession.

You see, as God's kids, we are not a part of that! You can refuse to participate! Did you know that? Read on, and I will tell you not only about the three harvests God has for His people but how you can be a part of them.

The First Harvest

Harvest number one is being blessed, even in the middle of a recession. In the Great Depression of the 1930's, more people became millionaires than at any other time. Similarly, God is going to do some incredible things in this hour.

> **We need to be blessed so we can be greater blessings to others.**

The reason we need to be blessed is so we can be greater blessings to others than ever before. We've got to fund the spread of the Gospel around the world, and we can't fund the Gospel if we can't pay our rent.

The Second Harvest

The second harvest coming on the land is the harvest of miracles. The Lord said we are going to see more miracles between now and the time Jesus comes than in the past two thousand years.

Personally, I know about miracles. I am a living, walking, breathing miracle myself, and I know beyond any doubt that miracles are for today. I was a Moslem businessman, left to die with shingles, blisters, chicken pox, a temperature of 107.6, and brain damage.

As a Moslem, I cried out for help. But Mohammed never showed up. Allah never came.

But Jesus of Nazareth walked in my room, and He saved me, healed me, delivered me, and set me free. So believe me, I know about miracles.

I love what the Apostle Paul said: *"My speech and my preaching was not with enticing words of man's wisdom, but in demonstration of the Spirit and of power" (1 Corinthians 2:4).*

4

You see, the world needs to see the power that is inside of us—God's miracle-working power.

My wife is also a living miracle. She was blind, paralyzed, and crippled with multiple sclerosis. Her hands were twisted up, and she had no feeling on the right side of her body.

When she was diagnosed with MS, an incurable disease in the natural, doctors said she would be a cripple for the rest of her life. But even at that time, I knew one Scripture well: *"So then faith cometh by hearing, and hearing by the word of God" (Romans 10:17).*

You may not know this, but the opposite is also true: fear also comes by hearing. That's why you've got to stay away from the media; you've got to listen to the Word more than you listen to the TV. The spirit of fear will get all over you, so don't listen to all that stuff.

I got some tapes on healing and played them by my wife's bedside twenty-four hours a day, seven days a week, for two straight years. She kept hearing the Word and hearing the Word and hearing the Word. It's wonderful when you speak the Word, but it's even more wonderful when it speaks to you!

But you can't live by another person's revelation. It's got to become *your* revelation to bring your revolution!

> **It's got to become your revelation to bring your revolution!**

After two years of listening to the Word 24/7, I can testify that my wife's eyesight came back. In fact, God restored every part of her body!

The doctors had said, "You'll never be able to have a baby." But Jesus said, "Get pregnant."

That baby we couldn't have just turned fourteen years old.

Oh, yes, miracles are for today!

My entire family is a miracle. The devil tried to kill all three of my boys, but they're all serving the Lord Jesus Christ today. The devil was actually successful in trying to kill my natural brother in London, England. He died in Westminster Hospital. As a Moslem, they took his body to the morgue, and he was on his way to hell.

But we started praying in Tulsa, Oklahoma, and after several hours of prayer, *God raised him from the grave.*

I was doing a conference in Orlando, Florida, when I received a call from my brother-in-law, who said that my sister was rushed to the hospital. She had a major infection, her lungs had collapsed, her kidneys and bladder weren't functioning, and her heart wasn't beating properly.

They put her on life support, and the doctors gave her less than a five percent chance to live. They said she would not live for twelve hours.

The doctors wanted to let her die. I refused to let that happen. I flew there and spent a week with her, and we prayed. You see, as God's kids, we've been given authority and power. Jesus said, *"All power is given unto me in heaven and in earth" (Matthew 28:18).* A few verses later, He said that He is with us always. Jesus gave us His power when He gave us Himself, so we started to exercise that power in my sister's life.

Despite what those doctors said, she went home. Her bladder, kidneys, lungs, and heart are working fine, and she has been healed.

Miracles are for today, my friend—no matter what the media reports about the economy!

The Lord told me to put all these miracles in our magazine, *Miracles Today*, and send a million of them out for free. So we've been sending them out all over the world, and we have received testimonies of people being healed reading the Word and the testimonies.

Stop listening to recession talk. God is giving ideas to Christians to step out, because He needs a vehicle to bless you through. One man listening to our CDs on the teaching of the Kingdom and God's blessing recently related to me that he has had an 1,800 percent growth in his business.

Let me tell you, that is also a miracle. We need miracles like this one, miracles in our finances. But you won't see that if you're listening to fear instead of faith!

The Third Harvest

The third and final harvest, however, is a harvest of souls.

As we follow the principles of God's Word as opposed to the principles of the world, we will increase and abound during this time that the world calls a "recession."

My spiritual father, Brother Kenneth Copeland, recently gave a prophecy. I have included it in this book, because I am confident that it will greatly encourage you to prepare to receive God's abundance rather than the world's recession!

Prophecy by Brother Kenneth Copeland

This is what the Lord is saying:

Don't pay any attention or make any plans based on what the media is saying or what the politicians say. Stand on My Word in John 16. Pay attention to Me. I, the Holy Spirit, will obey verses 13-15[i]. I will show you things to come. I will lead you through troubled times. I already have the plan for you. It is very good. Follow it. It will not only get you through, it will place you in a very high place—a rich place, a strong place of victory.

You will have to discipline yourself and be diligent to listen to Me. All the other voices will have a plan, a word, an idea for your future and security. Don't listen to the Babylonian system. It has fallen apart.

My system is stronger than ever. My Kingdom is flourishing, and the blessing is the place to be. Keep your eyes on My Word. Listen to it. It will guide you and I will perform it. Love Me and love My people, as I have loved you. Walk in it. Love never fails and neither does My plan.

Be very cautious to stay completely clean from covetousness. First Timothy 6:10[ii] must live in the forefront of your thinking. If you will do these things and continue therein, you will come into your wealthy place—a place lifted up, a place in Me already planned and prepared for you now. Here, not in heaven, not yet, but it will seem like heaven right in the midst of all the trouble. And you will be able to reach out to untold numbers of suffering people with the Good News of the Gospel.

I'm coming very soon, sooner than you think. Keep your eyes on Me, and you will get the job done.

When I got a hold of Kenneth Copeland's prophetic word, I said, "I got it! I'm going to have the greatest year of my life."

You are going to have the greatest year of your life as well! Read on, and I will tell you how.

---

[i]JOHN 16:13-15: *"However, when He, the Spirit of truth, has come, He will guide you into all truth; for He will not speak on His own authority, but whatever He hears He will speak; and He will tell you things to come. 14 He will glorify Me, for He will take of what is Mine and declare it to you. 15 All things that the Father has are Mine. Therefore I said that He will take of Mine and declare it to you."*

[ii]1 TIMOTHY 6:10: *"For the love of money is a root of all kinds of evil, for which some have strayed from the faith in their greediness, and pierced themselves through with many sorrows."*

Chapter 2
Demonstrating the Gospel

Are you ready to follow God into the best year of your life, no matter what the media says is going to happen? Then let us take the first steps together by looking at what Jesus had to say about the world's way and God's way—the difference between the world and the Kingdom of God.

In *Matthew 4:17* we read, *"From that time Jesus began to preach, and to say, 'Repent: for the kingdom of heaven is at hand.'"*

This quote comes from the beginning of Jesus' ministry. One of His first words was "repent." "Repenting" does not mean remorse. It comes from two words: "re" of course means "again," and "pent" comes from the old English word "penthouse," which means on the top. So "repent" means *it's time for you and me to get back on top!*

> "Think differently, for the government of God is beginning."

The English word is actually from the Greek word "*metanoeo*," and it means to transform your thought process, change your mind, and think differently.

Why did Jesus say we are to think differently? *"For the kingdom of heaven is at hand."*

One translation says, *"Think differently, for the government of God is beginning now."* That's what Jesus was talking about. He was saying that the governing influence and principles of heaven have now arrived. We will now have power over our environment. Instead of being under the circumstances, circumstances need to be under us. We are now more than conquerors and overcomers. In Christ Jesus, we triumph.

Jesus is not "the King of the Church" and not even "the King of the Christians." He's called "the King of kings."

It's time for us to rule and reign together with our Lord as kings in this life.

I want to show you in the Scriptures that regardless of what the economy of the world is doing, God can bless you in the middle of it. I am not talking about Elohim, the God of the laws of the universe under the Jewish understanding.

> **The Kingdom is what we are to establish on the earth, while the blessing is the manner in which we establish it.**

I am talking about El Shaddai, who parted the Red Sea three miles wide, who stopped the sun in the middle of the day, who turned water into wine, and who raised the dead. You see, El Shaddai *surpasses* all the laws of nature. There is nothing that He cannot do.

Now, I want to talk about El Shaddai and what He wants to do for you.

God's Kingdom—which Jesus was speaking about—and God's blessings are totally connected. The Kingdom is *what* we are to establish on the earth, while the blessing is the *manner* in which we establish it.

Let us look at a Scripture that connects the two.

Matthew 4:23 says, *"Jesus went about all Galilee, teaching in their synagogues, and preaching the Gospel of the kingdom, and healing all manner of sickness and all manner of disease among the people."*

The Gospel of the Kingdom is that they don't have to be sick anymore, and by healing and blessing these people, Jesus actually demonstrated the Kingdom.

Healing is actually part of the blessing. You can't tell me you're blessed if you are sick. Come on, that's not being blessed.

The blessing is the manifestation of the Kingdom on the earth.

Here's another way of looking at it: the Kingdom is where we are going. Blessing is how we are going to get there. Kingdom was brought through the blessing.

To have the greatest year of our lives, we have to bring the Kingdom of heaven to the earth.

Jesus said, "I'm preaching the Kingdom." What was He doing? *Luke 4:18* tells us: *"The Spirit of the Lord is upon me, because he hath anointed me to preach the Gospel to the poor."* Jesus was preaching the Kingdom. Jesus is saying the Kingdom is, "The poor don't have to be poor anymore."

Not only that—Jesus goes on to say, *"He hath sent me to heal the brokenhearted, to preach deliverance to the captives, and recovering of sight to the blind, to set at liberty them that are bruised."* Jesus is saying the Kingdom is, "The sick don't have to be sick anymore."

When the Kingdom comes, all of this will happen.

Jesus never once said, "The Holy Ghost is upon Me so I can run the aisles!" Jesus is in you to bless you, but the Holy Ghost is in you to bless others.

People come to me and say, "Pray, Brother Nasir. I want more anointing." I always ask them, "What did you do with the last batch?" Was anyone saved? Did God heal anyone through you? Deliver anyone? That is the purpose of the anointing.

What Is This Gospel?

Jesus was demonstrating the Kingdom, and He was preaching the Gospel. So what was this Gospel? We know it is the Good News, but why?

Galatians 3:8 says, *"And the Scripture..."* The word "Scripture," as used in this verse, has a capital "S." Why would it have a capital "S"? I studied this, and I asked the Lord, "Lord, why would it have a capital 'S'?"

He said, "Because I was talking about Jesus."

"And the Scripture [Jesus], foreseeing that God would justify the Gentiles by faith, preached the Gospel to Abraham beforehand." Who was it that preached? Jesus. What did He preach? Let's find out. He preached to Abraham, *"In you all the nations shall be blessed"* *(Galatians 3:8).*

> **The Gospel was and is a Gospel of blessing.**

So what was this Gospel saying? **Be blessed!** What was Jesus saying to Abraham? Be blessed. All the nations in the world will be blessed because of you! So the Gospel was and is a Gospel of blessing. Sight to the blind is a blessing. Freedom to the captives is a blessing. It is a Gospel of blessing.

If you are going to preach the blessing, look at the next verse. *"So then those who are of faith are blessed with believing Abraham"* *(Galatians 3:9).* You have to be in faith.

You cannot separate faith from the blessing.

A lot of people are not in faith and they are praying, "Bless me, bless me, bless me, Lord." No! Who is blessed? Those who are "of faith." This isn't just those who have accepted Christ. That's not what "faith" means. In the Greek it is the word "*pistis*"—those who believe. They are the ones who are going to get blessed. Faith is critical to the blessing.

Now, let's look at *Luke 4:14,* which says, *"And Jesus returned in the power of the Spirit into Galilee."* The Amplified Translation of this verse says: *"Then Jesus went back full of and under the power of the [Holy] Spirit."*

The Holy Spirit is involved in the blessing. In fact, you cannot separate the Holy Spirit from the blessing.

Luke 4:1 says, *"And Jesus being full of the Holy Ghost returned from Jordan."* Why is this so important? Let's read it from *The Amplified: "Then Jesus, full of and controlled by the Holy Spirit."*

If you want to walk in the blessing, you have to give up control. You can't do your own thing anymore. You are going to have to obey God.

Blessing is always conditional on obedience.

So we can't separate faith from the blessing, and we can't separate obedience to the Holy Spirit from the blessing. They are critical. In fact, you will find out that disobedience actually stops the blessing and cancels the blessing in your life. When we disobey, the curse is loosed. That is what happened with Adam. Because of disobedience, man lost the Eden blessing. They lost dominion, authority, provision, protection—they lost everything.

You will lose the game if you disobey. Disobedience disqualifies stewardship. God cannot trust you with increase when you have not

Disobedience schedules lack in your future.	been obedient with the first portion. **Disobedience schedules lack in your future.**

We give the devil too much credit for some of the struggles we are facing. Many times it has nothing to do with the devil. We are reaping the repercussions of disobedience.

The Lord Shall Arise Upon You

I did a study from Genesis to Revelation, and every time there was a plague, pestilence, famine, or drought, God's people who obeyed His Word and obeyed His voice prospered and were blessed in the middle of a recession. It will be no different in this hour.

Isaiah 46:10 says, *"Declaring the end from the beginning, and from ancient times the things that are not yet done, saying, My counsel shall stand, and I will do all my pleasure."*

God declared the end from the beginning. He saw the end first and then went back to the beginning and declared it. God sees recessions before they show up. He's never caught off guard. He knew what was going to happen with the financial institutions in America long before it happened. God made a way out.

There are three keys that will get you out of the recession. Every recession from Genesis to Revelation was stopped when the people obeyed God's Word and voice. When there was darkness in Egypt, there was light in Goshen. When there was pestilence in Egypt, there was prosperity in Goshen. You have to get it rooted on the inside of you that God always makes a way of escape from every recession. In fact, He wants to prosper you in the middle of a recession.

Isaiah 60:1 says, *"Arise [from the depression and prostration in which circumstances have kept you—rise to a new life]! Shine (be radiant with the glory of the Lord), for your light has come, and the glory of the Lord has risen upon you!"* (AMP)

The word *"arise"* in this verse means to arise from the depression and the prostration in which circumstances have kept you. We have to change our thinking. We should expect to have the greatest year of our lives. Recession time is opportunity time! Now is the time to arise. The wealth you have been waiting for has not been sent back to heaven—it is still here! Throughout the Bible, that wealth was always transferred to God's people during troubled times.

Isaiah 60:2 says, *"For behold, darkness shall cover the earth, and dense darkness [all] peoples, but the Lord shall arise upon you [O Jerusalem], and His glory shall be seen on you"* (AMP).

The recession is bringing darkness into the world. People are in fear because they are listening to the world and not the Word. The spirit of fear did not come from God. He gave us the spirit of power, love, and a sound mind *(2 Timothy 1:7)*. We are not supposed to be afraid of a mortgage meltdown. Recessions should never touch us. God is our source, and He is not going under. There are more buying opportunities in a recession than any other time.

Isaiah 60:3 says, *"And nations shall come to your light, and kings to the brightness of your rising"* (AMP).

What will cause you to be so bright that nations come to you? *Isaiah 60:4-5* tells us:

Lift up your eyes round about you and see! They all gather themselves together, they come to you. Your sons shall come from afar, and your daughters shall be carried and nursed in the arms. Then you shall see and be radiant, and your heart shall thrill and tremble with joy [at the glorious deliverance] and be enlarged; because the abundant wealth of the [Dead] Sea shall be turned to you, unto you shall the nations come with their treasures.

(AMP)

The wealth of the Dead Sea refers to the wealth of the nations. The wealth transfer described in this verse is available for you. Go ahead and help yourself. The world's wealth is coming to you, but you are going to have to do three things.

Psalm 115:12-15 says,

The Lord has been mindful of us, He will bless us: He will bless the house of Israel, He will bless the house of Aaron [the priesthood, He will bless those who reverently and worshipfully fear the Lord, both small and great. May the Lord give you increase more and more, you and your children. May you be blessed of the Lord, Who made heaven and earth!
(AMP)

God is thinking about you. His blessing upon your life has nothing to do with any recession. We can walk away from any recession prosperous and healed. But the wealth transfer cannot occur if we do not do our part.

Psalm 133:3 says, "*It is like the dew of Hermon, descending upon the mountains of Zion; for there the LORD commanded the blessing—life forevermore.*"

"Commanded" is past tense. God is not going to command the blessing—once was enough. The blessing has been commanded over you. God saw the end from the beginning. He already placed your wealth right here on the earth. FedEx does not pick up from heaven. Your blessing is already here. God knows everything about you, including what struggles you are facing in your life. He has already made provision for your every need. Long before any recession showed up, He planned a way out for you.

Don't Stay in the Dark. Get in the Ark!

Let's go back to the book of beginnings, the book of Genesis, where in chapter six a serious "recession" was about to hit planet earth. It was so serious that it killed everybody—*everybody*—except for one family who never participated in it. That was Noah's family.

Why didn't he participate in that recession? Because God said, *"Make yourself an ark..."* (*Genesis 6:14*). God didn't say, "I will make an ark for you." He said, "You make it, Noah."

When the flood hit, Noah and his family were doing just fine, because they were in the ark. You can't have one foot in the world and one foot in the ark. It doesn't work that way—you are either onboard, or you are drowning in the waters.

Recently, I was sharing with some people about getting onboard the ark. It is actually a lot like going through airport security—when you go to an airport, you have to go through the metal detectors, and if you have any metal on you, you can't go through.

Similarly, you can't get on the ark if you try to walk through with unforgiveness. If you try to go through with unforgiveness, alarms go off. You can't build an ark and then try to bring unforgiveness onboard with you. You have to get rid of it, and the same is true of any other sin that's a part of your life. You have to repent and get back on top so you can pass through onto the ark God wants you to build.

The Bible says, *"Be ye holy; for I am holy"* (*1 Peter 1:16*). So we're going to have to get rid of some stuff to get into the ark.

But while it is time to repent and rid ourselves of covetousness and greed, it is also time to see how God has planned our blessing from the beginning. Let's take a look at His plan, the way it started in Genesis.

Chapter 3
Blessed from the Beginning

You are still reading, so you must want to know more about God's blessing. In fact, we have been blessed from the beginning. So let us talk about the blessing, beginning in Genesis chapter one.

Genesis 1:26 says,

> *God said, Let Us [Father, Son, and Holy Spirit] make mankind in Our image, after Our likeness, and let them have complete authority over the fish of the sea, the birds of the air, the [tame] beasts, and over all of the earth, and over everything that creeps upon the earth.*
>
> (AMP)

Why is it important to know that it was "complete authority"? It means that God didn't keep any of it for Himself. When He gave complete authority, He meant "complete authority." In other words, when you ask God to do something for you on planet earth, you already have that authority! God gave it to you!

Remember, after Jesus rose from the dead, He said, *"All power is given unto me in heaven and in earth" (Matthew 28:18)*. Jesus gave it to the Church, so we as believers have it. So asking God to change your situation is a wasted prayer. It's time for you and me to walk in the authority He has given us.

Looking back at *Genesis 1:26*, I also want you to notice that when it says we have complete authority *"over all the earth,"* that includes your home—your dominion.

Man had authority and the blessing. I'll show you how it operates. *Genesis 1:28* says, *"And God blessed them."* The word "blessing" as used in this verse is the Hebrew Chaldean word *"brakah,"* and it means not just empowered to prosper, but it means **liberal prosperity**. That's what God gave us.

God gave us liberal prosperity.

How did God bless mankind? He spoke a blessing over us, just as Melchizedek spoke a blessing over Abraham. When the blessing comes on you, it's because somebody who has the authority to transfer it and speak it has transferred it to you.

God spoke to Noah exactly the same way when the ark finally came to a rest after the flood. *"Be fruitful, and multiply"* He told them *(Genesis 9:1)*. The same thing God said to Adam in *Genesis 1:28*, He told Noah eight chapters later: *"Be fruitful, and multiply."* God blessed their productivity.

So what does that tell us? Blessing is transferred through words.

When God speaks something, it is created. That's how He created the universe. He spoke it into existence. So the moment God said it, the empowerment to be fruitful came upon Adam. After God spoke it they could be fruitful and multiply.

So since we're talking about blessing, would it not be good to know how you become fruitful? The word "fruitful" is the Hebrew Chaldean word "productive" or "creative." In other words, the blessing is on you, so start to multiply, start to produce, start to create, by what you believe and what you speak.

God rested on the seventh day, but it wasn't because He was tired. He doesn't get tired. Why did He rest on the seventh day? Because God turned over the creating process to us—to you!

So God has created Adam, and He's in the Garden. But God was not done creating humanity.

> **God turned over the creating process to us—to *you!***

Look at what God says in *Genesis 2:18: "And the LORD God said, 'It is not good that the man should be alone.'"* Do you know what Adam said? "God, what does 'alone' mean?" That's all he knew—fellowship with God. He didn't know anything else. So God says, *"I will make him a helper comparable to him."*

Now, how did God make man? Out of dirt. So guess what God did? He went back to the drawing board, which was the dirt, to make Adam a helper. *"And out of the ground the LORD God formed every beast of the field, and every fowl of the air; and brought them unto Adam to see what he would call them"* (v. 19).

Notice God *brought* the dirt forms to Adam. He did not lead them. In other words, those dirt forms were not alive yet. Adam was in charge of deciding what they would be and then calling them forth. God formed a piece of dirt and carried it over to Adam. God was trying to make a companion for Adam. One by one, God presented the options to Adam!

He picked up the first piece of dirt, walked over to Adam, and said, "Adam, the authority and dominion on planet earth to create is now with you. So this piece of dirt isn't going to be what I call it, because I have given you that authority. This piece of dirt will be what you call it."

And so Adam looked at that piece of dirt and said, "The neck is long. I think that one is going to be a giraffe." And the moment he said that, that piece of dirt started walking away. Then God brought another bit of dirt and put it in front of Adam and said, "What do you think of this? Whatever you call it, that's what it will be, because you have dominion and complete authority. Start creating. Be fruitful, and multiply. Whatever you call this next bit of dirt, it will become that."

Then God asks, "What about this one?" Adam's response, "That nose is too long. I think I'm going to call it an elephant." The animals became what Adam named them. He was operating under the blessing, being fruitful and multiplying.

Genesis 2:19 says, **"Whatsoever Adam called every living creature, that was the name thereof."** Adam was operating under the blessing. He was being fruitful and multiplying, because he had obeyed the Word.

Every recession from Genesis to Revelation was stopped when the people followed these three steps. You must believe the Word and speak it out, obey the instruction, and sow the seed that God directs.

Psalm 141:3 says, **"Set a guard, O Lord, before my mouth; keep watch at the door of my lips"** (AMP).

You can create a recession in your life through your mouth! Stop agreeing with the world's report. If you turn off the news, you might start speaking the right things. If false information is entering your ears, eventually it will exit out your mouth. At that point you have given life to something that has no business operating in the life of a child of God.

When you set a guard over your mouth by making sure whatever you are saying agrees with God's Word, then you will experience heaven on earth while the world is in a recession. Tell yourself that you always hear the instruction of God and you always obey the Word. Never say anything contrary to the Word. There is no point in believing the Word but then speaking something else.

Christians, beware of using the words "never" and "always" in a negative way. Put a guard over your mouth.

Psalm 19:14 says, *"Let the words of my mouth and the meditation of my heart be acceptable in Your sight, O Lord, my [firm, impenetrable] Rock and my Redeemer"* (AMP).

Let your words honor God. "Meditation" means, "to think, consider, ponder, and mutter." "Heart" means "mind" in this context. We have to think on the right things in order to say the right things.

Now, let's go to *Genesis 2:8*, which says, *"And the LORD God planted a garden eastward in Eden; and there he put the man whom he had formed."*

God is a sower. He took heavenly seed and planted it into the earth. That is how the Garden of Eden came about. Then God turned all authority over to man. The only person who could plant from that point on was not God, but Adam. All God could do was give Adam seed. *"And God said, 'See, I have given you every herb that yields seed which is on the face of all the earth, and every tree whose fruit yields seed; to you it shall be for food'"* (Genesis 1:29). Adam had the choice of whether to sow it or not.

Genesis 1:11 says, *"And God said, Let the earth put forth [tender] vegetation: plants yielding seed and fruit trees yielding fruit whose seed is in itself, each according to its kind, upon the earth. And it was so"* (AMP).

God spoke to the earth and commanded it to bring forth harvest. The earth has no choice in the matter. When man sows seed into the earth, harvest has to come. If seed never touches the earth, it is wasted seed. God cannot violate His own Word. Once He told the earth to bring forth harvest, it was a settled issue.

Seed in the ground creates a harvest. God does not create the harvest; man does it through the seed that was given to him. If man's seed never hits the ground, no harvest will ever come. Be thankful Adam did not eat all of the seed! God gave Adam seed for a purpose, and the seed still remains in the earth.

Genesis 8:22 says, *"While the earth remains, seedtime and harvest, cold and heat, summer and winter, and day and night shall not cease"* (AMP).

The earth is still here! Therefore, seedtime and harvest is still in effect. Whether or not we ever see a harvest depends upon our sowing. God is not giving harvest. There are no shipments coming from heaven. The harvest is here; it's not in heaven. Seedtime and harvest is a law established by God.

If you want to see a harvest in the middle of a recession, you will be required to sow seed. There is no other way to get a harvest. Prayer will not bring it. There are no shortcuts to this system.

I travel all over the world and see Christians struggling. They want to pray in their harvest. Harvest does not follow prayer; it follows a seed. You will not escape this recession if you don't adhere to the rules.

Second Corinthians 9:10 says, *"And [God] Who provides seed for the sower and bread for eating will also provide and multiply your [resources for] sowing and increase the fruits of your righteousness [which manifests itself in active goodness, kindness, and charity]"* (AMP).

God cannot give you the harvest. The blessing, the abundance, and the overflow only comes one way when man uses his authority on the earth. The word "earth" refers to the solid part of the region including the occupants. When man sows, he reaps a harvest that comes from the earth.

Since God cannot give you harvest, how does He get involved? God issues seed to the man who is a sower. A sower gets a steady flow of seed. Along with that seed, God issues instructions. God already gave you the authority and spoke to the land. He helps us out by telling us what seed is going to bring in the harvest we need. His instruction will cause us to win the game every time. He cannot play the game for us, but He can give us counsel. He gives the Word, the instruction, and the seed, but He cannot give the harvest. **When we obey the instruction, the harvest has no choice but to show up.**

> **When we obey the instruction, the harvest has no choice but to show up.**

The moment you obey God and sow seed, God has a legal right to speak to men to walk into your life and pour into your bosom the harvest of that seed. Men are not going to show up with your stuff until you give. Give and it shall be given unto you.

Adam Messed Up

Adam failed to stay in the blessing. He sinned, and, in effect, got off the ark of blessing God had given him.

Adam messed up because he disobeyed God, and when he disobeyed, he lost the blessing.

How did Adam lose the blessing? *Genesis 3:1* tells us, *"Now the serpent was more cunning than any beast of the field which the LORD God had made."* The serpent was the devil, Lucifer, an archangel of God. Before Adam was ever created, Lucifer had taken one-third of the angels and started a rebellion against God. Jesus said he fell from heaven like lightning *(Luke 10:18)*.

Now remember, God had said to Adam, *"Be fruitful, and multiply, and replenish the earth, and subdue it"* in *Genesis 1:28*. Adam wasn't supposed to subdue the animals; he was supposed to subdue Lucifer who, as Satan, was in the Garden before he was.

Genesis 3:1 said that the serpent was more cunning than anything else the Lord had made, and he said to Eve, *"Has God indeed said, 'You shall not eat of every tree of the garden'?"* He was asking, "Did God really say that?"

The next verse says, *"And the woman said to the serpent, 'We may eat the fruit of the trees of the garden.'"* So she knew what God had said.

Verse three says, *"But of the fruit of the tree which is in the midst of the garden, God has said, 'You shall not eat it, nor shall you touch it, lest you die.'"* But this is where the trouble starts, because that isn't precisely what God said.

Be careful, because man has a tendency to add to the Word. Back in *Genesis 2:16-17*, it says, *"And the LORD God commanded the man, saying, 'Of every tree of the garden you may freely eat; but of the tree of the knowledge of good and evil you shall not eat, for in the day that you eat of it you shall surely die.'"* What did God say? He said, "Don't eat it."

Yet somehow when Eve is relating what God said, God saying, "Don't eat it," got changed. God never added, "You can't even touch it."

But in *Genesis 3:3*, Eve said, *"But of the fruit of the tree which is in the midst of the garden, God has said, 'You shall not eat it, nor shall you touch it, lest you die.'"* God never said that.

He said, "The whole garden is yours—but don't eat from that one tree there." You would not die by touching it, but you would die by eating of it. That's all God said—don't eat it. But Eve wouldn't even go near the tree, because she thought, "If I touch it, I'm going to die." But that's not what God said.

In *Genesis 3:5*, the serpent says, *"For God doth know that in the day ye eat thereof, then your eyes shall be opened, and ye shall be as gods, knowing good and evil."*

But she was already made in the image and likeness of God. Not only was she like God, she had all authority on the whole planet. She didn't need any more authority.

Eve was made in the image and likeness of God; she didn't need any more authority.

The same way, people who don't know who they are in Christ or who don't know their authority in Him are waiting for God to do something that He has already done.

The tree was in the middle of the Garden, but the next verse says, *"And when the woman saw that the tree was good for food,"* (v. 6) as though she hadn't really seen it before. Perhaps up to this point, she had never seen the tree. Otherwise, she would have seen that it was good, but she never saw it.

That tells me that the serpent led her into the center of the Garden, to this tree. She didn't go there by herself; Satan led her.

So when she saw it—because the devil led her there—what happened? It says,

And when the woman saw that the tree was good for food, and that it was pleasant to the eyes, and a tree to be desired to make one wise, she took of the fruit thereof, and did eat, and gave also unto her husband with her; and he did eat.

(Genesis 3:6)

The devil didn't bring the curse to the world, because he didn't eat from the tree. Who ate of the tree of the knowledge of good and evil? Eve did. Who else ate of the tree? Adam did.

Now, who released the curse on the earth? Adam and Eve ate of it. They stepped out of the blessing.

You see, the fruit was not ripe. God was going to teach them about the knowledge of good and evil and blessings and curses at a later time, when they were ready. But they took something that wasn't theirs, and that's what released the curse.

Now, look at what happened. *"And the eyes of them both were opened, and they knew that they were naked"* (v. 7). Now, wait a minute. They've been naked all these years. It wasn't a problem yesterday. Why did it become a problem today?

The glory had lifted. Now they could only see with their natural eyes. They could no longer see with their spiritual eyes. God is a Spirit, and they walked and talked with Him in the cool of the day—until now!

Adam and Eve lost the blessing. They sinned—they disobeyed God.

Can I give you a definition of sin, because sin will cause you to lose the blessing? Sin is error or failure, but here's the definition I like best: **sin is violation of a divine command.**

> **Obedience brings the blessing, while disobedience removes the blessing.**

When you disobey God's Word, you are in sin. When you disobey the Holy Ghost's directive, you are in sin, and that's what happened. The moment Adam and Eve disobeyed God, sin entered.

Let's put this very simply: Obedience brings the blessing, while disobedience removes the blessing.

God released the blessing on Noah. Then with Abraham, God cut a covenant and released the blessing on him. Then Jesus went to the cross, and the Bible says, He died on the cross. And in dying, He redeemed us from the curse of the law and returned us to the blessings of Abraham.

The same blessing God placed on Abraham, the father of faith, is now on you and me! Would it be a good idea to look further at what activates the blessing? I'd say so!

Chapter 4
Faith and Obedience
Activate the Blessing

Remember our questions: what activates the blessing? Faith and obedience.

What stops the blessing? Disobedience and fear.

The world is trying to feed you the spirit of fear through the media. In my house, we don't turn on the television. We don't listen to any bad news. You may be thinking, "But don't you want to know what's going on around the world?" No. Why? It can change me by letting in fear. I don't want fear in my life, and I don't want disobedience.

For me and my house, we're going to read the Word. Whatever the Word says, we're going to take God literally. And He said He's going to bless me—even in the middle of a recession.

Staying in faith and obedience is the most important thing you can do right now.

We are going to prosper in this recession. We are not going to fail or struggle. We're going to prosper. Why? Because we're going to put our faith in the Word, and we're going to stay in obedience to the Word and to the Holy Ghost.

Those are the most important things you can do in your life right now—stay in faith, and stay in obedience.

God blessed my ministry with a plane, and we were flying over the United States on one occasion. I looked out the window, and I saw this cloud, and then I saw an opening in the cloud. I said, "Lord, look! The sun is shining in that opening." You could see the trees, the grass, the leaves, and the houses far below. When I said, "Look, the sun is shining right there," the Lord said, "No, you're wrong, son. The sun is shining everywhere, but only those people are seeing the benefit of it."

The Son is shining everywhere—the blessing is there to be had. But if you're not walking in faith and obedience, you may be under the cloud instead of *in* the Son.

This could be the year of the extravagant blessing, and as long as you are out of position, you're not going to walk in it. Lord, show us how we can get in position to walk in the fullness of Your blessing—the extravagant blessing!

Paul—Loaded with "Extravagant" Blessings

Let's go to Romans, chapter 15, and let me tell you a story about a gentleman named Paul. He went through some recessions, and he prospered in all of them.

Paul is writing to the Christians in Rome. He says these words: *"And I am sure" (Romans 15:29)*. He was sure of something. He was rooted, grounded, and absolutely convinced of something. What was it that he was so convinced of? *"But I know that when I come to you, I shall come in the fullness of the blessing of the Gospel of Christ."*

He was not fazed by recession or troubles within the Roman government. It didn't matter what was going on. He was saying, "I am convinced because I know my God, and when I come to Rome, I am going to arrive loaded!" The word "fullness" happens to be the Greek word that means "bounty, filled up to the fullest measure." One version of the Bible translates it, "extravagant."

He was saying to them, "When I come to you in Rome, I am coming in the extravagant blessing." Was he sure? Was he convinced? Did he absolutely believe it? Yes, he not only believed it, he spoke it!

Now, let's look at Paul's journey to Rome. Paul said, "I'm coming loaded," but what happened to him on his way to Rome?

Acts 27:39-44 says:

When it was day, they did not recognize the land; but they observed a bay with a beach, onto which they planned to run the ship if possible. [A bad storm was going on.]

And they let go the anchors and left them in the sea, meanwhile loosing the rudder ropes; and they hoisted the mainsail to the wind and made for shore. [Because of the storm, they headed into the shore. They wanted to get away from the storm.]

But striking a place where two seas met, they ran the ship aground; and the prow stuck fast and remained immovable, but the stern was being broken up by the violence of the waves. [Bad news! The ship is destroyed.]

And the soldiers' plan was to kill the prisoners, lest any of them should swim away and escape. [Worse news for Paul, one of the prisoners.]

But the centurion, wanting to save Paul, kept them from their purpose, and commanded that those who could swim should jump overboard first and get to land, and the rest, some on boards and some on parts of the ship. And so it was that they all escaped safely to land. [Paul loses everything owned on that ship, yet he said, "I'm coming in the extravagant blessing."]

Paul Reaches Malta

Acts 28:1 says, *"Now when they had escaped, they then found out that the island was called Malta."*

Paul and the other prisoners swam for their lives. Paul lost everything. He, along with the other prisoners, arrived on the beach soaking wet. In the next verse we read, *"And the natives showed us unusual kindness; for they kindled a fire and made us all welcome, because of the rain that was falling and because of the cold"* (v. 2).

This does not sound like Paul is coming in the "extravagant blessing." But it gets worse!

Acts 28:3 says, *"But when Paul had gathered a bundle of sticks and laid them on the fire, a viper came out because of the heat, and fastened on his hand."*

This was not a good day for Paul. He's going from bad to worse! And just when you think it is as bad as it can get—loss, cold, and bitten—the people think he's a murderer and refuse to let him close to the fire. In verse four, it says, *"So when the natives saw the creature hanging from his hand, they said to one another, 'No doubt this man is a murderer, whom, though he has escaped the sea, yet justice does not allow to live'"* (Acts 28:4).

Have you ever lost everything in a recession? Have you had to swim for your life, figuratively speaking? Have you ever been cold and shivering, thinking it couldn't possibly get worse, when a poisonous serpent grabs a hold of you in an effort to kill you? And then the ones who had seemed to offer some comfort think we are cursed for the things that are happening and refuse us access to what aid they offer.

Many of us can identify with this, which was just one of Paul's many trials. This was no "recession" he was facing; it wasn't an economic downturn in the tent-making business that threatened to cramp the quality of his lifestyle.

This is not a good day for Paul—this is a day that should have, in the natural, claimed his life.

But let's look at what Paul did, because he did indeed get to Rome.

Shake It Off!

Acts 28:5 says that he shook off the snake that bit his hand. Paul was able to do this because he knew the anointing was in him. Paul knew the Greater One abided on the inside of him and that no weapon formed against him could prosper. When you understand the anointing that is in you, no recession the world produces can touch you. You actually believe that you can do all things—in good times or bad times. Weapons can be formed, but they cannot prosper against you. You have to be so rooted in the Word that circumstances cannot affect you. When you belong to the Kingdom of heaven, recession cannot touch you.

If a poisonous viper could not kill Paul, surely a recession is not going to hurt you. You have the same anointing that he had; it is the same Holy Ghost in you that was in Paul. I don't care what is going on in the world—you can shake it off! Shake off the mortgage crisis; shake off the credit crisis; shake off the economic crisis.

You and I are not a part of this world. We are a part of the Kingdom of heaven. And I've got good news! Heaven has no problem with its economy, and it has no recession. Shake off the world. Let it go. As for me and my house, we are living by the Word.

"He shook off the beast into the fire, and felt no harm" (v. 5). Remember, the islanders thought Paul was a murderer because of being bitten by the poisonous viper. How serious is it when a viper bites you? I wonder what I would have done in that situation. I wonder if I would be so rooted and grounded in God's Word—who I am in Christ and the authority that has been given to me—that I could shake it off? Are you that grounded?

Are we that grounded in the Word that when the world says, "This is the greatest recession in the last sixty years," we can say, "I shake that off"?

Paul was sure of his God. Are you that sure of your God? Are you that sure of El Shaddai, the all-sufficient One? Are you that sure of whom you serve? Are you that sure of your Provider? Are you so sure of Him that you could shake off this recession, and say, "This recession cannot touch me"? Never forget this: weapons *will* be formed against you, but only you can make the decision that they will not prosper. If you don't make that decision, I've got news for you: they will prosper.

> **Weapons *will* be formed against you, but you decide that they will not prosper.**

Paul said, "Not even a poisonous viper can keep me from coming to Rome with an extravagant blessing." He just shook it off.

Paul didn't waver, and his circumstances didn't change—he was still shipwrecked, cold, and bitten by a snake. He was sure of his God, and it affected his world.

Now, look at what happened. *"However, they were expecting that he would swell up or suddenly fall down dead. But after they had looked for a long time and saw no harm come to him, they changed their minds and said that he was a god" (Acts 28:6).*

This has to be the fastest murderer-to-god transition I've ever seen. One minute he's a murderer; the next minute he's a god. This is awesome!

Do you know why the viper couldn't kill him? Let me give you a clue. He had the Holy Ghost. Let me give you another clue. He who was in Paul was actually greater than the serpent that tried to cling to his hand.

He who is in you is greater than any recession, any poisonous serpent's bite. Are you rooted and grounded in that? Are you sure that the anointing in you is greater than anything the world can bring against you? Until you get that rooted and grounded, media tales of fear and woe will still mess you up.

The viper couldn't kill Paul, because no circumstance could take away that which God had given him. You can lose everything like Paul did, but there is one thing no one can take from you, and that's *the anointing*. No sea could take it from Paul, no shipwreck, no water, no rain, and no viper could take it from him. No one can take your anointing and your blessing if you'll shake it off and stay grounded in your God, El-Shaddai!

Let's read on and see how God used Paul's obedience to bless not only him, but a whole island! What would you say if God wanted to use you as a blessing? I'd say that's one of the biggest reasons He blesses us!

Chapter 5
Paul Obeyed. God Blessed.

So we were reading of Paul's stay on the island of Malta. Not exactly voluntary, was it? He was shipwrecked, bitten by a snake, and refused shelter, not to mention losing everything he had.

But Paul did not let his circumstances dictate his faith. Let's read on to see how God used Paul's continuing obedience.

The story goes on that in that same region was the estate of a leading citizen of the island, Publius—we'll call him the president of the Island of Malta. And this head honcho, instead of reviling Paul as a prisoner and maybe a snake-bitten murderer, received him courteously for three days.

Why would the president of the island receive a prisoner named Paul? Because he demonstrated the anointing. Paul lived when he should have died, and other people saw God's power in him. So the president says, "Come to my house and tell me what happened."

In the middle of circumstances far greater than any recession, Paul found his circumstances changing; once cold and shipwrecked, he is now the guest of Publius of Malta. And it was because of He who was in Paul and the power of the anointing. Powerful people will open doors for you, even during hard times, because God will prosper you, even when in the middle of a recession.

Now, it gets even better. Verse eight says, "*And it happened that the father of Publius lay sick of a fever and dysentery.*" The moment Paul found out about Publius' father, he knew what to do. He didn't take three weeks to figure out what he should do.

Paul didn't keep the anointing to himself. His mind wasn't fastened on what he had lost or perhaps the viper-fang marks on his hand. He wasn't thinking about what he had lost or the blessing he did or didn't have. His thoughts turned immediately to whom he could *bless*.

> **Nobody can take your anointing unless you give it up.**

He lost all material possessions, but he didn't lose the anointing. Nobody can take your anointing unless you give it up.

Paul's first response was, "A man is sick, but he won't remain sick in my presence, because I know who I am. I know who is living in me, and I know what authority and power I walk in. I know what anointing is inside of me. Sickness, you can't stay in my presence."

When Paul found out that Publius' father was sick, he went looking for him. "*Paul went in to him and prayed, and he laid his hands on him and healed him*" (v. 8).

Do you remember what happens when you lay hands on someone—how the blessing is transferred? You activate the law of contact and transmission. There's a transmission of the anointing going on. The moment that transmission occurred, Publius' father was healed.

Remember, no one can take the anointing from you, but you have a responsibility to use it. You have to make a decision to change your world with that anointing. You cannot just hang on to the anointing. The anointing grows when you give it away. Christians are struggling because they have been holding on to the anointing. We are supposed to give it away. Sometimes when I pray for pastors, I pray that the teaching anointing that is on me will get on them in its fullness. I have no problem giving away my anointing because I understand how it increases. You can never give away too much. If you hang on to everything you already have, you will never grow.

Hanging on to what you've got is not a work of faith. When you hang on, you are trusting in yourself and your riches when you should be trusting in God. Learn to give it away as an act of faith.

> **Hanging on to what you've got is not a work of faith.**

Releasing the anointing makes your faith complete. Letting go lets God know that you are not trusting in what you've got. When you are not afraid to give it away, God will move you into a greater level of anointing because you have demonstrated your faith.

Your seed is your evidence of your faith. What you are saying through your release of the anointing is that you trust God. **Until you are ready to release something, nothing will change in your life**. When you are ready to bless others, blessings will overtake you! God doesn't just want to flow to you; He also wants to flow *through* you. He needs vessels to flow His blessings through. If He cannot flow through you, He is going to have to find somebody else.

If you give freely of the anointing and if you will start using it to be a blessing everywhere you go, something will happen in your life. **When the anointing is upon you, it is to change the world around you**. We are supposed to administer the blessing everywhere we go, and that's what Paul was doing.

Now, what happened when Paul did this? *"So when this was done, others also, which had diseases in the island, came, and were healed"* (v. 9). When the serpent can't kill you, the world finds out. When a recession can't get your joy, the world finds out. When the mortgage meltdown can't affect you, the world finds out. When a credit crunch can't affect you, the world finds out.

These people learned of the anointing on Paul, and they brought their sick ones to him to be healed. They said, "I don't know what this man has, but I want some." Paul believed the Word and obeyed the instruction. He laid hands on the sick, and the sick recovered.

Don't ever discard the anointing. You will see restoration of everything if you will administer the anointing and in turn bless others.

Look at what happened. *The Amplified* version says, *"They showed us every respect and presented many gifts to us, honoring us with many honors; and when we sailed, they provided and put on [board our ship] everything we needed"* (v. 10).

The Scripture says "they" provided gifts for Paul, meaning there were many people who gave into Paul's ministry. Jesus said that when you give, men would give back to you in good measure, pressed down, shaken together, and running over. After Paul released the blessing, men showed up with some gifts.

Paul had said, "I'm coming in the extravagant blessing." There was nothing the devil could do to stop it. No shipwreck could stop it. The wind and waves couldn't stop it, and neither could a poisonous viper.

As long as you do not let go of the anointing and are a blessing everywhere you go, nothing can stop it. They gave Paul so much stuff that it took a crew of men to carry it onto the new ship.

Paul had said, "I am sure of this one thing. When I show up in Rome, I am coming loaded." Having lost everything, he still would arrive fully supplied!

In fact, Paul received so many gifts that it took a crew of men to carry it all aboard ship! He had lost it all, but it could not stay away for long because the anointing got it right back.

> **Even after losing everything, Paul still arrived loaded with blessing!**

Everything was restored, and Paul left the island loaded. Recession had no power over Paul. This blessing resulted from his obedience. He believed the Word and obeyed the voice of God. We must believe that God can bless us in any recession.

The gifts that Paul received were already here on the earth just waiting for him to show up on the island of Malta. None of that wealth showed up from heaven. All of the wealth for Paul was already laid up for him, but had he disobeyed, he would have missed out on it all. This is an example of a wealth transfer. The wealth of Malta became the wealth of Paul.

Your wealth is not in heaven either. You will find it here on the earth when you hear the Word, obey the voice of God, and release your seed. Wealth is waiting for you on the other side of obedience.

Now, watch this: believe it or not, it gets even better. *"And after three months we departed in a ship of Alexandria, which had wintered in the isle* [no coincidence, right?], *whose sign was Castor and Pollux"* (v. 11). Of all the ships in the Alexandrian fleet, there was one ship that was absolutely the finest, the sleekest, the most beautiful, and the fastest. It had two heads on the front—those of Castor and Pollux, the mythical Twin Brothers.

Can you picture the Christians, having received a letter from Paul saying he was coming with an extravagant blessing, waiting at the port? And they saw a ship pull up filled with the prisoners, but no Paul. They saw another prisoner ship pull up, and again no Paul.

One guy says, "Look! The finest ship in the Alexandrian fleet is coming into port. Who's that in a robe standing on the bow? Is that Paul? He really is coming loaded!"

Yes, this man who was once a wretchedly cold prisoner, a viper-bitten, penniless shipwreck survivor, arrived in Rome on the finest ship in the fleet loaded with blessings he received on Malta. All because he was sure of this one thing: "If I will not give up the anointing, and I will be a blessing everywhere I go, I will arrive in the extravagant blessing."

No recession is going to do anything nearly as bad to you as the events that happened to Paul, but you'd better be sure of this one thing: you are going to arrive on the other side loaded. This is going to be a year of extravagant blessing!

In a good economy, even the sinners prosper. But in this situation and time, there will be a separation. The sinners will struggle, and the believers will rise! When they see the anointing, the sinners will start looking for us. "Who is this God you serve who is prospering you?"

You have the same anointing as Paul. Don't let go of it; no one can take it from you. Be a blessing everywhere you go with that anointing, and God will prosper you.

You will rise and arrive in the fullness of the blessing!

Obedience: Key to Extravagant Blessing

No weapon formed against us can prosper, but we have to obey the Word and obey God's voice. The key is obedience. If there was one thing Paul knew, it was how to obey the voice of the Holy Ghost. Remember, as soon as he arrived at Publius' house, the Holy Spirit said, "Heal this man." Why? Because the Holy Spirit came to walk and talk and minister through us.

> **Obedience opens the door to His blessing.**

You have the same anointing that Paul had. You don't have a lesser anointing than Paul. You don't have a lesser Holy Ghost than Paul. The One who is in you is greater than any recession.

But you've got to get the revelation inside of you and say, "I will not quit. I cannot be stopped, because I know who I am. I know who my daddy is, I know who is living inside of me, I know the name that I have, and I know the authority that I walk in."

We aren't just saying, "We won't participate in this recession." We are *demanding* that we aren't going to participate, because we know who we are. Those who will follow the Word and obey the Holy Spirit will prosper in this time, because God always blesses obedience.

Some people think God is simply moved to action by the tragedy of people's plights. While there is no denying His mercy, God has a system for meeting our needs. He isn't in the need-meeting business; He's in the instruction business, and obedience opens the door to His blessing.

Chapter 6
Blessing Follows Obedience

Obedience, you read in the previous chapter, is the key to extravagant blessing. And while God does want to meet our needs, He doesn't simply exist to do so.

Remember this statement: **God never meets a need. He gives an instruction, and blessings follow.** Let me explain.

> God doesn't fulfill a need. He gives an instruction.

Moses and several million Jews stood on the banks of the Red Sea, in need of deliverance. There are mountains on one side and the sea in front of him. He looks back, and the Egyptian army is coming to kill him and the Israelites. Most of us know this story, but I'm going to make another statement that I pray will shock you.

God didn't part the Red Sea—He gave *Moses* an instruction to do so.

"Help me, Lord. We've got three million of Your people, and the Red Sea is before us! The Egyptian army is coming to kill us. Help! Help, Lord!"

God's answer is very interesting: *"And the LORD said to Moses, 'Why do you cry to Me? Tell the children of Israel to go forward'"*

(Exodus 14:15). Then He goes on and says, *"But lift up your rod, and stretch out your hand over the sea and divide it. And the children of Israel shall go on dry ground through the midst of the sea"* (v. 16).

God says, "You see that staff in your hand? Put it over the water."

Moses probably asked, "Anybody else up there? The rod isn't going to do anything. That's just a piece of wood. No, bring Your angel. Surround us. Get us out of here. Lift us up. Do something."

And God says, "Put the stick over the water, son."

Had Moses disobeyed God's instruction, we wouldn't be reading about it today. Remember what I said? God doesn't fulfill a need. He gives an instruction.

Need of the Blessing

Returning to our text in Acts from the previous chapter, we see that God was going to make sure Paul arrived loaded.

God's instruction to us in the New Testament is that we are to lay hands on the sick and pray for their recovery. This was His instruction to Paul. God said, "Go lay hands on Publius' father and everybody else who is sick. Don't worry about the other stuff. It will come. You just obey My instruction."

Need of Something Lost

"I lost my ax-head in the water. What am I going to do?" a servant asked Elisha in *2 Kings 6:5-6.*

I wonder if the prophet heard God say, "See that little stick over there?"

"Yeah."

"Cut it off and throw that in the water where the ax-head fell in."

"What? How's throwing the stick in going to help?"

"Throw it in the water, son."

"Really?" He threw it in the water, and the iron ax-head floated to the surface.

You see, God didn't just meet their need. He gave an instruction.

Need of Protection

In *2 Chronicles 20:1-30*, King Jehoshaphat said, "The army is arrayed against us, Lord. What are we going to do? I think we're going to go out and meet them. We are going to send our best soldiers."

"No, you are going to send the worshipers," God instructed.

"What? The worshipers? Come on, God. Get serious. Not the worshipers!"

But Jehoshaphat obeyed, and God set ambushes for his foes, and the enemies of Israel killed each other without the warriors of Judah swinging a weapon. And in fact, they then went down where the enemy armies had camped and they gathered the spoils for three days!

God didn't meet the peoples' need. He gave the king an instruction.

Need of Provision

At the wedding feast in Cana of Galilee in John Chapter 2, Jesus' mother told Him that they had run out of wine. She then told the servants to do whatever Jesus instructed them to do.

He told them to fill the pots with water and draw some out for the master of the feast. To these servants, this instruction no doubt seemed outlandish. But when the servants obeyed, the water became the best-tasting wine the master of the feast had ever tasted.

God didn't meet this need. He gave an instruction.

Need of Abundance

Simon Peter was going through tough times. His fishing business was struggling. "We've been fishing all night, Lord, and we caught nothing," said Peter.

"Put your nets over there for a catch," Jesus said.

"Jesus, now wait a minute," Peter could have complained. "You probably know a little about carpentry, You certainly know about the Word, but You do not have a clue about fishing! I've been a fisherman all my life. My daddy was a fisherman. My granddaddy was a fisherman. I know this lake. I'm telling you, the fish aren't biting. A fisherman would never put his nets out in the middle of the day. I'd get kicked out of the fishermen's association."

At this point, maybe Jesus gave him a stern look and Peter said, "But on your instruction, I'll do it." It made no sense, but Simon Peter obeyed and caught the biggest haul of his life.

Why? Because God didn't meet Peter's need. He gave Peter an instruction.

His provision will only be where He directs you to go. You cannot go fishing on the wrong side of the lake and expect His provision. Peter made that mistake. When your business is going broke, you need to make a change! Jesus gave Peter the right instruction as to where to cast his nets for a huge catch. Peter's recession was not a fish problem. The fish were always there. The problem was where the nets were being cast. God's provision for Peter was in a different part of the lake.

God commands the supply before the need ever shows up. You must be convinced that God commanded your provision during any recession long before it ever hit. God always makes arrangements ahead of time for you to experience His blessing, but if you step out of His perfect will, you will miss out on what He planned.

> **God commands the supply before the need ever shows up.**

The devil has never been able to cut off God's supply to His people. Only disobedience has the ability to cut off the supply.

Need to Fulfill an Obligation

Peter got another object lesson the day he came to Jesus and said, "Jesus, how are we going to pay our taxes?"

Jesus was so loaded, He could have given Peter the tax money. But when Peter asked about paying their taxes, Jesus said, *"Nevertheless, lest we offend them, go to the sea, cast in a hook"* (*Matthew 17:27*). At this moment Peter was probably thinking, "How many fish do I need to catch to earn enough money for the tax bill?" The answer was one!

Jesus continued and said, *"Take the fish that comes up first. And when you have opened its mouth, you will find a piece of money;*

take that and give it to them for Me and you." Fish don't eat coins in the natural! But Peter obeyed, and the coin was there.

Jesus didn't meet their need. He gave an instruction.

How Loaded was Jesus?

One of the twelve disciples was stealing from the money bag, and the other eleven guys couldn't figure it out. But as we said, Jesus was loaded. His stepfather, Joseph, was loaded—when about 99.9 percent of the people walked, Joseph probably drove a Mercedes donkey. Jesus' family were carpenters. They were contractors, and they probably had Ford work-donkeys, too.

So when the disciples of John the Baptist came and they asked Jesus, "Are you the One?" He showed them His miracles and took them to His house. Later He taught the people for three days. They were in church so long, they were passing out because of hunger. So Jesus said, "Disciples, go feed them." There were five thousand men, plus women and children—probably close to twelve thousand people—and not one disciple said, "We don't have enough money." They said, "There isn't a store close by." Had there been a store, Jesus apparently had petty cash enough to feed all of those people. Money wasn't an issue for Jesus.

When He needed an upper room, He got it. When He needed a brand-new donkey, He got it. Sounds like a new car to me. It was no issue. Judas tried to stop Mary from sowing her seed. "What? That perfume was one year's wages. It could feed the poor." But Jesus said, "No, the poor will be with you always. Let her sow her seed."

People have problems with money, but Jesus never had a problem with money. He did fine. When they took Him to the cross, His robes were so expensive, they didn't have any seams. You've never seen Versace suits without seams. They cast lots for Jesus' robes because they were so expensive.

Obey I AM

This may seem shocking, but did you know that they never crucified Jesus? When the soldiers came that night, it was a garrison of six hundred soldiers. They asked, "Are you the One they call Jesus of Nazareth?"

Guess what Jesus said? "I AM." You know what "I AM" means? El Shaddai, the all-sufficient One. And the moment He said, "I AM," six hundred soldiers fell backward.

No, they didn't crucify Jesus. *He laid His life down.* Legions of angels could have carried Him away. But Jesus had received a command from His Father, and He was obeying it—so we could walk in blessing!

Just obey!

Your blessing is on the other side of obedience. If you don't obey God's instructions, you will miss it. Obedience brings the blessing, while disobedience cancels it. Your provision, your blessing, is waiting for you on the other side of your obedience. The instruction you obey is the future you create.

> **The instruction you obey is the future you create.**

Just do it. Why? Because God isn't into meeting needs; He's into giving instruction, expecting you to obey, and then blessing you.

If there ever was a time the Body of Christ needs to know, hear, and obey the voice of the Holy Spirit, this is it. When you obey the Spirit of God, you will prosper in the midst of any recession. Hear

His instruction, and obey. Blessing *will* follow. You can be sure of this!

In the next chapter, we will look at God's Kingdom established and the blessing prevailing. I'm sure you'd like to see His blessings prevail in your life!

Chapter 7
Blessed Are the Humble

At the beginning of this book, I included Brother Kenneth Copeland's prophecy for the following year. I took it personally, and I said, "This is for me. I don't care what the media is saying; this year is going to be the greatest year of my life."

But if the Lord tarries, it doesn't have to end there. Each year can be the greatest year, but there are some keys that we are going to have to follow for it to happen, so I've broken it down for you.

Remember, we are establishing God's Kingdom on this earth, and we are empowered to do so through God's blessing. With that fixed in your mind, let's look at God's Kingdom established and the blessing prevailing.

In *Matthew 5:3*, Jesus is speaking: *"Blessed are the poor in spirit: for theirs is the kingdom of heaven."* You can't separate the blessing from heaven. In fact, if we went on and read all the other verses in this same chapter, you will see, "Blessed is so-and-so." Why? Because they have come into the Kingdom. "Blessed" and "Kingdom" are tied together.

I wanted to know what the Greek word for "blessed" is and what it meant. Let me read it from *The Amplified Bible*: *"Blessed (happy, to be envied, and spiritually prosperous—with life-joy and satisfaction in God's favor and salvation, regardless of the outward conditions)."*

> **We are supposed to be blessed in the midst of any condition.**

We are supposed to be blessed in the midst of any condition. Being blessed has nothing to do with what is going on with the economy. It has nothing to do with shrinking economies. It has nothing to do with the mortgage meltdown. It has nothing to do with the credit crunch. In the middle of all the outward conditions, we are blessed.

Verse three says, *"Blessed are the poor in spirit."* Many come to the wrong conclusion about this verse and think it has to do with prosperity. But it is very simple. Jesus didn't give us a complicated Gospel. "Poor in spirit" means "the humble."

God stays far from the proud, but He gives grace to the humble *(Proverbs 3:34)*. Regardless of what is going on in the world, my Bible says, *"Where sin abounded, grace did much more abound" (Romans 5:20)*. Who is grace coming to? The humble. Who gets blessed? The humble.

Again, *The Amplified* sheds more light, saying blessed are *"(the humble, who rate themselves insignificant), for theirs is the kingdom of heaven!" (Matthew 5:3)* To possess the Kingdom of heaven and blessings in a recession, you have to walk in humility. So the blessing and the Kingdom are connected. You can't separate the two of them. "Kingdom" is what we get. "Blessing" is how we get it, or the empowerment.

Three Keys to Blessing

There are three keys that are critical to the blessing: **B**elieve the Word. **O**bey the Holy Spirit. **S**ow your **S**eed. Those three keys are critical if we are going to see the Kingdom established here on earth and if we are going to walk in the blessing.

Key 1: Believe the Word

First, how did God transfer the blessing? He spoke with words. Why? Faith comes by hearing. And what must we hear? The Word. So to walk in the blessing, you must walk in faith.

While I was studying this, the Lord gave me revelation. He said, **"It isn't the Word that will change your life. It is the Word believed."** What does this tell us? The Word will not help us if we don't believe it. Most Christians are walking around with Bibles, but they are sick, broke, and struggling. What's the deal?

> It isn't the Word that will change your life. It is the Word *believed*.

Owning a Bible doesn't change your life—it's just that simple. You must read it and believe it! *Believing* the Word will bring change to your life. You cannot let the world feed you nonsense and then wonder why the Word is not working for you. You have a choice to either believe God's Word or the world's word.

Another meaning for the word "belief" is *faith*. Faith is the Word believed. To live by faith means to live by the "Word believed." Walk, talk, and act as though the Word is so.

God's Word says you are going to be blessed with all things freely *(Romans 8:32)*. He did not spare His own Son, so why would

He withhold any good thing? The Word says that God receives pleasure in our prosperity *(Psalm 35:27)*. We have to draw a line in the sand. Beyond a shadow of a doubt, we have to stand on the Word that says no recession formed against us can prosper. Recessions can be formed, but they do not have the power to affect us. Go with the Word. Be one of those crazy Word believed people.

James said, *"But be doers of the word, and not hearers only, deceiving yourselves" (James 1:22)*. You must walk in the Word believed. You must also be a doer of the Word.

Can you imagine if Adam said, "What are You talking about, God? Be fruitful and multiply? I don't believe that." We wouldn't read about Adam anymore. He had to hear the Word, and then he had to believe it.

If God says to you, "Be fruitful and multiply," then He has transferred to you the ability to be fruitful and multiply. It can't just be the Word. It has to be the Word *believed*.

Key 2: Obey the Holy Spirit

Romans 8:14 states: *"For as many as are led by the Spirit of God, they are the sons of God."* That means you can be born again, yet not truly be called a son. You could be Spirit-filled and tongue-talking, but God may still not call you a son.

The qualification for sonship is that you have to be *Spirit-led*.

The word "led" in the Greek literally means an animal pulled by a cord. That means you can't do your own thing anymore. If we are going to be prosperous and blessed in this recession, we have to give up control and let the Holy Ghost lead us.

In this verse, the word "son" is the Greek word "*huios.*" In this context, "*huios*" means "mature sonship." One translation of the word *huios* is "one who looks like and operates like his parents."

Romans 8:16 says, *"The Spirit Himself bears witness with our spirit that we are children of God."* "Children" here is not the word "*huios.*" It's the word "*teknon,*" meaning "little baby or toddler." You could be a Christian 47 years, and God may still call you "a little toddler."

We have to know, hear, and obey the voice of God, not as toddlers but as mature sons and daughters. There is zero option in this!

Verse 22 says, *"For we know that the whole creation groans and labors with birth pangs together until now,"* not for the "*teknon,*" the little toddlers, but for the sons—those who know who they are, who walk in the fullness of the Word, and who are obedient and led by the Spirit of God.

Deuteronomy 28:1-6 says,

If you will listen diligently to the voice of the Lord your God, being watchful to do all His commandments which I command you this day, the Lord your God will set you high above all the nations of the earth. And all these blessings shall come upon you and overtake you if you heed the voice of the Lord your God. Blessed shall you be in the city and blessed shall you be in the field. Blessed shall be the fruit of your body and the fruit of your ground and the fruit of your beasts, the increase of your cattle and the young of your flock. Blessed shall be your basket and your kneading trough. Blessed shall you be when you come in and blessed shall you be when you go out.

(AMP)

> **The instruction must be obeyed before the blessing will flow to you.**

Being blessed coming in and going out is contingent upon your obedience to the voice of the Lord your God. **The instruction must be obeyed before the blessing will flow to you.** Let this be so rooted in you that you refuse to do your own thing anymore. Every decision must be Spirit-led. God knows where to move your chess piece in the game of life.

God has been trying to communicate with man for all time. Jesus was sent to the cross so we could obtain access to the throne of grace. Open communication with God will always cause you to know what instruction will win the game.

Job 36:11 says, *"If they obey and serve Him, they shall spend their days in prosperity and their years in pleasantness and joy"* (AMP).

The condition to spending your days in prosperity is obeying and serving God. Recession is not a factor in your prosperity. The economical climate cannot determine your prosperity. Only your obedience will bring pleasant years of joy. Choosing to obey God brings great reward.

Job 36:12 says, *"But if they obey not, they shall perish by the sword [of God's destructive judgments], and they shall die in ignorance of true knowledge"* (AMP).

The alternative is not very pleasant! The disobedient perish for lack of knowledge.

Isaiah 1:19 says, *"If you are willing and obedient, you shall eat the good of the land"* (AMP).

The good of the land is not going to show up someday. It is already here, waiting for you to chow down! Solomon was a trillionaire, the richest man to ever walk the earth. He did not take his wealth with him when he died. Those riches are still here. All of Solomon's wealth remains here on earth. None of it was shipped out. **The wealth is ready to come into the hands of the obedient.**

> **Wealth is ready to come into the hands of the obedient.**

God didn't come to live in you and bring His pillow. He's not looking for somewhere to sleep. He's looking for somewhere to take over. He wants to talk through your words, through your ministry, through you.

So the second condition to the blessing is you have to obey and be led by the Spirit of God.

Key 3: Sow Your Seed

There is something else that is needed to flow in the blessing. Adam started to create through his words, and that's how all the animals became what they are today. It's because of what Adam did, not because of what God did.

In *Genesis 1:11* God said, *"Let the earth bring forth grass, the herb yielding seed, and the fruit tree yielding fruit after his kind, whose seed is in itself, upon the earth: and it was so."* What was God doing? He was speaking to the earth. He was saying, "Earth, when you get seed, I want you to cause that seed to grow. Not only that, I want you to cause that growth of seed to produce more seed, and it will be of the same kind as the original seed."

Once God speaks something, even God cannot violate His Word.

How did God create the Garden? *Genesis 2:8* says, *"And the LORD God planted a garden eastward in Eden."* This is Elohim. He is speaking the laws, and He won't violate His laws. But, He has the right as El Shaddai to override them.

What did He plant? He planted seed. Once the seed hits the ground, the earth is commanded. It has no choice but to obey the command of God. I don't care if you are a Moslem, a Hindu, or a Buddhist. If you put seed in the ground, the earth is going to give you a harvest.

God commanded that whatever was planted in the ground would reproduce, so what did God plant in the ground? Seed. Here comes the next question: Where did He get the seed He gave Adam in *Genesis 1:29*?

The disciples came to Jesus one day and they said, *"Teach us to pray."* He said, "Okay, here's a good prayer: *'Our Father which art in heaven, Hallowed be thy name. Thy kingdom come, Thy will be done'"* *(Matthew 6:9-10)*. Where? *"On earth as it is in heaven"* (v. 10).

When we pray this prayer, what are we really saying? "God, can You make earth look like heaven?"

So, how did God make the earth look like heaven? God took heavenly seed and planted it in the Garden.

> **Adam's job was to make the rest of planet earth look like the Kingdom of heaven.**

If you want to grow a plant, you get a seed from the plant you want to reproduce and put it in the ground. God took heavenly seed, planted it in the earth so that the earth would look like heaven. Then God gave Adam the job of taking care of the Garden of Eden. (By the way, "Eden" actually means "a spot of God's presence." That's why Adam could walk and talk with God in the cool of the day.)

Adam's job was to make the rest of planet earth look like the Kingdom of heaven—like the seed God planted.

God gave authority and dominion of all of planet earth to Adam. God started the Garden, put Adam in it, and said, "I want the rest of planet earth to look like the Garden of Eden. You have dominion, authority, and rulership over the whole planet."

So, *first* Adam needed the Word, because the Word is faith. It will work in your life. *Second*, he needed the Holy Spirit to guide and direct him. You have the Holy Spirit. And *third*, Adam needed the same thing that God used to start the Garden—seed.

You Are the BOSS!

These three things are critical if you want to prosper abundantly. You are going to have to believe the Word, obey the Holy Spirit, and sow some kind of seed.

A good way to remember this is with the word "BOSS." If you want to be boss in this economy, you must Believe, Obey, and Sow Seed.

The key here is that the measure of your giving is going to affect the measure of your blessing. You cannot be stingy and expect overflow in your life. God's level of blessing is contingent upon your measure of seed. Generous givers experience abundant grace and favor. You will never suffer lack when you give liberally.

Remember, the Word of God must be believed, the instruction of the Holy Spirit must be obeyed, and the right seed must be sown. The right seed is the one that the Holy Spirit directs. Then we can be the *boss* in any recession!

We have been waiting on the Lord to change our situation, but we are the ones that have to do it. We have to be the *boss!*

There is good news in the Kingdom of God. This is a wonderful time for the Church. You have to stop looking at a recession as something negative and start looking at it as something positive. There are more opportunities during a recession than any other time for wealth transfers.

Prospering in a recession depends upon your perception. If you think you can't, then you can't. On the other hand, if you think you can, now you have created an opportunity.

When many people are in the middle of a recession, they are hoping that it does not last very long. I don't care if it lasts six years! I want as many opportunities as I can get my hands on. Throughout the Bible, every time there was a recession, there was also a wealth transfer. We should be going after every opportunity that is out there. Do you know what poor means? **P**assing **o**ver **o**pportunities **r**epeatedly! Poverty is written all over the person that passes over opportunities repeatedly in a recession. It's time to seize opportunities.

Why should the Body of Christ be paying full price for real estate? We ought to be paying half-price! Why should we pay full price for stocks? In a recession you can get them for half-price! In a recession we have the greatest opportunity for wealth transfer to take place.

God wants us to arise and shine. When darkness covers the earth, prosperity comes to God's people *(Isaiah 60)*. God has commanded the blessing. It is already done. The way we walk in prosperity while the rest of the world is in recession is to follow the three steps and be the BOSS:

1) **B**elieve the Word

2) **O**bey the instruction

3) **S**ow the **S**eed

Disobedience Derails Blessing

Faith and obedience through sowing seed activates the blessing, even in the middle of a recession. If you remember that statement the rest of your life, you can avoid being a part of any recession that comes. The Bible was not meant to be complicated.

As I studied and followed all the blessings, I couldn't find one that didn't have a seed attached to it.

What did God give to Adam? He gave him seed. God says, *"Behold, I have given you every herb that yields seed which is on the face of all the earth, and every tree whose fruit yields seed; to you it shall be for food" (Genesis 1:29).*

The Holy Spirit was critical to all of this. Adam had the ability to spread the Garden of Eden all over the earth. All he had to do was be fruitful and multiply.

But one thing caused him to lose it all: disobedience.

> **Adam could have spread the Garden of Eden all over the earth. But one thing caused him to lose it all: disobedience.**

Like Noah, you must take God at His Word and do things God's way, not the world's way—you can't have one foot on the ark, and one in the world. You can't do it the world's way and wonder why God's blessings aren't happening in your life.

God does not build arks—He instructed Noah to build the ark to provide for him and his family. And it wasn't just an economic recession that hit Noah's world—it was a flood that killed everyone except for the Noah family.

Do you think God might have known that the recession of the late '20s and '30s was coming? Do you think He knew beforehand about the recessions we have faced? He saw the end from the beginning. He knew about each one long before it came. I believe He will tell His people, "Build an ark!" The big question is, will anyone listen? I believe He was telling people, "Build an ark," but was anyone listening? Disobedience will cause you to be stuck in a recession.

Disobedience caused Adam to lose the blessing. He decided to obey Satan's word instead of God's Word. That's exactly when sin entered. Remember the definition I gave you for sin? It is a violation of a divine command.

So are you obeying God's commands or the devil's? Are you listening to the negative reports of the media or are you reading and hearing the positive reports in the Word of God?

As for me and mine, we're walking as obedient sons that obey our Father. And, like a father, God knows what is best for us. In fact, sometimes He puts conditions on receiving His blessing. We will look at what those are and how they affect the blessing He wants to give you.

Chapter 8
Conditions for Blessing

We have been reading about how God wants to bless us, but He is not a fairy godmother. He is our Father, and as a father, He loves us but also wants us to do the right thing. Obedience, we've established, opens the doors to blessing.

In *Deuteronomy 28:1*, God gives us the condition for receiving His blessings: *"Now it shall come to pass, if you diligently obey the voice of the LORD your God, to observe carefully all His commandments which I command you today, that the LORD your God will set you high above all nations of the earth."*

How do you walk in the blessings? It has to do with whose voice you listen to, obey, and follow. But we know there is a condition because of the word "if." Perhaps you thought all the blessings would come if you just prayed. No, praying and saying won't bring the blessing. Obeying is the key to receiving the blessings.

The next verse tells us what will happen *if* we obey the Holy Spirit. *"And all these blessings shall come upon you and overtake you, because you obey the voice of the LORD your God."*

> **A failure to receive the blessing was proceeded by a failure to obey.**

If you obey God's voice and the instruction He gives, you will be meeting a condition. So if you aren't obedient, the blessing isn't going to come on you and overtake you. We could say it this way—**a failure to receive the blessing was proceeded by a failure to obey.**

"But you don't know what I'm struggling with," you might say. "It's not fair!" Have you ever gone through a trial that God didn't know about? I thought He saw the end from the beginning.

Some people go another direction and try to blame God. "Well, He wanted me to go through that trial," they say. "He wanted me to have that cancer," or, "He wanted me to lose my job." But God doesn't teach us that way. Never! He teaches through the Word—our failures are the result of us failing to obey.

Some others try to put the responsibility on God for not telling us about every specific attack from the enemy that will affect us. I don't know about you, but my Bible says He will show us things to come *(John 16:13)*. He is faithful, even when we are faithless *(2 Timothy 2:13).*

> **We fail to receive His blessing because we're not hearing and obeying!**

We fail to receive His blessing because we're not hearing and obeying!

Weapons can be formed against us, but my Bible says none of them should prosper. But with many Christians, the weapons are being formed, and they *are* prospering. Why? We haven't listened to the voice of the Lord our God.

If you are losing a battle, it takes humility to say, "God, maybe it's not You. Did I miss it somewhere along the road?" Blessings come to the humble.

Blessing is connected with obedience. Receiving the blessings has a lot to do with our obedience! God's blessings are on us right now. We have been redeemed from the curse of the law, and we have been redeemed to the blessings of Abraham. Yet the key to receiving God's blessings is obedience.

Dr. Yonggi Cho of Seoul, South Korea, has the biggest church in the world—800,000 to a million people in one church. One day Dr. Cho was asked, "What is the key to your success?" He gave two very simple keys: "I *pray* and then I *obey*." People were waiting for a profound response, but that's all Dr. Cho said—*pray and obey*. That was it. He built a million-member church by following those two things. That was the key to everything that he did. He wouldn't do anything until he prayed, and then he obeyed.

So what are the three keys to receiving God's blessing? Be led by and obey the Holy Spirit, believe and act on the Word, and you must have a seed. And what frustrates the blessing on your life and causes you to fail to receive it? Disobedience. Like Dr. Cho, we must pray, and we must obey whatever instructions God gives us.

Abram Prospered in a Time of Famine

Let's go through some famine situations in the Bible. What I am about to share with you is heavy, but you can handle it. Let's go to Genesis: *"Now the LORD had said to Abram: 'Get out of your country, from your family and from your father's house, to a land that I will show you'"* (Genesis 12:1).

Does God meet needs? Or was He giving Abram an instruction? We'll come back to this verse, but if we skip down to verse ten, we read that there was a famine. Was this famine a shock to God? Did He know a recession was coming?

God told Abram what to do—He gave him an instruction. What if Abram had said, "I don't want to leave my daddy's house. I want to hang out here. I don't want to obey You. I'm quite happy doing my thing"? He would have lived in the middle of that famine.

But the good news is that he obeyed God, and we read the results in verse two where God tells Abram what would happen: *"I will make you a great nation; I will bless you and make your name great; and you shall be a blessing."*

God had spoken to Abram: "Leave your house, follow Me, and obey My voice." Do you know what was going to happen when the famine hit or how convenient it was for Abram to obey God? We don't, but we know what God said: "I'm going to make a great nation out of you, and not only that, while this famine is going on, I'm going to bless you, and make your name great. And I'll make you a *blessing.*"

You and I were always meant to be administrators of God's blessing—He always intended us to distribute it, as Adam was to spread the Kingdom of God out from the Garden. It was never a "bless *me*" club. God always intended it to be a "bless and flow through me" situation. You were always meant to be a *blessing.* The blessing was supposed to come on you and then go on to the rest of the world *through* you.

People are hungry, and you are going to feed them. People have no clothes, and you are going to clothe them. People are suffering, and you are going to be there to help these people, because you bring His blessing with you. You are bringing the Good News. People are poor, and you are going to show them how to abound. People are sick, you are going to pray and show them healing.

You bring the blessing. You are a blessing administrator. But you must obey!

You bring the blessing. You are a blessing administrator. But you must obey!

It goes on: *"I will bless those who bless you, and I will curse him who curses you; and in you all the families of the earth shall be blessed"* (v. 3). People down your street ought to be blessed because they live on your street. People at your workplace ought to be blessed because you work there. Your relatives ought to be blessed because they are hanging out with you. Why? Because through you, God is blessing others.

I have good news and bad news for you. The good news is that you are the Body of Christ. The bad news is God doesn't have a spare to use in your place. You're it! If He can't flow through you, who is He going to flow through? You're not just to be blessed; you're supposed to be a blessing.

God gave Abram an instruction. Did he obey the instruction? Did he stay in his daddy's house or did he leave? Thank God, he obeyed, giving us a model of faith and blessing.

When you obey God, you start to flow in the blessing. Abram got up and left his daddy's house (v. 4). He did it by faith, but it was obedience that caused this to happen.

Now, when he left his daddy's house, you have to remember, he didn't have much. He had a wife. He had his nephew Lot with him. But he didn't have a whole lot of stuff. We know he didn't have a house. He probably didn't have much furniture. So he's going on this long journey with everything he has, probably in one suitcase.

In a short time, things changed dramatically for a guy that left his father's house with so little. *Genesis 13:2* says, *"And Abram was very rich in cattle, in silver, and in gold."* So what happened between leaving his daddy's house and *Genesis 13:2*? He got blessed in the middle of a famine.

How did it happen? Number one, he got the Word from God—an instruction. He believed the Word. God said, "If you leave your daddy's house and follow Me, I'm going to bless you." Did God keep His Word? Yes. Could God have kept it if Abram had never left his daddy's house? No.

You can't do your own thing and wonder why blessings don't come upon you and overtake you.

I have read this many times, but when I asked the Lord where the seed was, He showed me some things that were important.

Genesis 12:10-12 says:

Now there was a famine in the land, and Abram went down to Egypt to dwell there, for the famine was severe in the land. And it came to pass, when he was close to entering Egypt, that he said to Sarai his wife, 'Indeed I know that you are a woman of beautiful countenance. Therefore it will happen, when the Egyptians see you, that they will say, "This is his wife"; and they will kill me, but they will let you live.'

Abram thought, "If these Egyptians see I have this beautiful woman with me, they are going to kill me for her." So he told Sarai to say she was his sister (v. 13). I thought for many years that Abram lied, but he didn't. Both Abram and Sarai came from the same father, but each had a different mother. Sarai really was his sister—but we won't go there.

Now, watch this:

'Please say you are my sister, that it may be well with me for your sake, and that I may live because of you.' So it was, when Abram came into Egypt, that the Egyptians saw the woman, that she was very beautiful. The princes of Pharaoh also saw her and commended her to Pharaoh. And the woman was taken to Pharaoh's house. He treated

Abram well for her sake. He had sheep, oxen, male don-
keys, male and female servants, female donkeys, and camels.
(Genesis 12:13-16)

Abram came with one suitcase. So what happened? I know this is a little bit far-fetched, but get a hold of this. He came with Sarai. Now, don't do what Abram did—don't sow your wife as your seed. But that's exactly what Abram did. Sarai was taken to Pharaoh's house. Abram didn't have much when he showed up in Egypt, but he had a beautiful wife, and he wanted to stay alive, so now his beautiful wife ended up with Pharaoh.

But by sowing that seed, Abram got a serious harvest in the middle of a famine. Pharaoh got so excited that he decided to give Abraham some sheep, oxen, donkeys, camels, menservants and maidservants. What made Pharaoh give all that stuff to Abram? Sarai. Without Sarai, none of this would have happened.

Abram **believed the Word, obeyed the voice of God** to leave his father's house, and **sowed seed.** For a guy who started with nothing, Abram was very rich—in the middle of a recession.

Verse 17 says, *"But the LORD plagued Pharaoh and his house with great plagues because of Sarai, Abram's wife."* Do you know what the plague was that hit Pharaoh's house? The womb of every woman was closed. That was the plague. No one could get pregnant because of what happened to Pharaoh. That was the plague because of Sarai, Abram's wife.

So what happened next? Pharaoh finally figured it out. "None of my wives are getting pregnant. There's something wrong here. Maybe Sarai was not his sister."

And Pharaoh called Abram and said, 'What is this you have done to me? Why did you not tell me that she was your wife? Why did you say, "She is my sister"? I might have taken her as my wife. Now therefore, here is your wife; take her and go your way.' So Pharaoh commanded his men concerning him; and they sent him away, with his wife and all that he had.

(Genesis 12:18-20)

Abram didn't arrive with much, but he left blessed.

Genesis 13:1-2 says: *"Then Abram went up from Egypt, he and his wife and all that he had, and Lot with him, to the South. Abram was very rich in livestock, in silver, and in gold."*

Did Abram believe the Word? Did he obey the voice? Did he plant a seed? Notice here that the first thing that came back to him was his seed. Never be afraid to obey God. Whatever seed you are sowing, God gave it to you the first time, and He is about to give it back.

So Abram became very rich in the middle of a famine and recession.

But is Abram the only one to prosper in a time of famine? Let's read on and find out.

Chapter 9
Joseph's Obedience Created Israel's Future

We find yet another famine in *Genesis 47:13*: *"Now there was no bread in all the land; for the famine was very severe, so that the land of Egypt and the land of Canaan languished because of the famine."*

So was this famine a shock to God? I should think not.

God gave a vision to Pharaoh, and Joseph was the only one who could tell him what this vision was about. Joseph's interpretation of the vision revealed that there would be seven years of plenty and seven years of famine. God already saw it coming. Because Joseph interpreted the Pharaoh's vision, he was promoted out of the prison and was placed in the palace as second in command of all the land of Egypt.

In his new position, Joseph followed the direction of God. During the years of plenty, he stored up grain in preparation for the years of famine. While others were spending, he was storing up grain.

What happened when the famine hit? Only Pharaoh, because of Joseph, had barns full of food. This recession was no shock to God, and when it came, it was a serious famine for Egypt and Canaan.

Look at what happened in verse 14: *"And Joseph gathered up all the money that was found in the land of Egypt and in the land of Canaan, for the grain which they bought; and Joseph brought the money into Pharaoh's house."*

By selling grain to the people, Joseph eventually collected all the money in Egypt and Canaan, and he put the money in Pharaoh's treasury. But money runs out.

We read in verse 15, *"So when the money failed in the land of Egypt and in the land of Canaan, all the Egyptians came to Joseph and said, 'Give us bread, for why should we die in your presence? For the money has failed.'"*

They ran out of money, but the people of Egypt and Canaan still needed food. Joseph had a solution. *"Then Joseph said, 'Give your livestock, and I will give you bread for your livestock, if the money is gone'"* (v. 16).

> **Wealth is coming now to the ones who obey God's voice.**

Money is failing today. **Wealth is coming now to the ones who obey God's voice.** Verse 17 goes on to say, *"And they brought their cattle unto Joseph: and Joseph gave them bread in exchange for horses, and for the flocks, and for the cattle of the herds, and for the asses: and he fed them with bread for all their cattle for that year."*

The World's Wealth is Headed Your Way

Some Christians are going to become millionaires when recession comes, because they will obey the Holy Spirit. Again, more people became millionaires during the Great Depression than at any other time. It's time for that to happen to us. There has to be a separation. The world struggles when recessions come, but Christians can rise up and prosper. This is our time!

During recessions the man or woman with cash is king. You can pick up some real estate property, stocks, and businesses very cheaply. Joseph was in the same situation. He had what everyone wanted—food—which brought the wealth of the world to him.

We read on in verse 18, *"When that year had ended, they came to him the next year and said to him, 'We will not hide from my lord that our money is gone; my lord also has our herds of livestock. There is nothing left in the sight of my lord but our bodies and our lands.'"*

The money was gone. The cows, sheep, and goats were gone. The people had nothing left to sell but themselves. *"Why should we die before your eyes, both we and our land? Buy us and our land for bread, and we and our land will be servants of Pharaoh; give us seed, that we may live and not die, that the land may not be desolate" (Genesis 47:19).*

Everything was coming to Pharaoh, and he was getting richer from it. Why? Because a man of God obeyed the plan of God.

"And Joseph bought all the land of Egypt" (v. 20). Many of you are going to buy some farms, some commercial real estate and some homes. Get ready for what is going to happen, because you are going to obey the voice, you are going to believe the Word, and you are going to sow. Because you sow, God is going to bless you, and you are going to take that money and buy up your town.

All the land in Egypt now belonged to Pharaoh because of Joseph. Why? Because he was following God's plan. *"And Joseph bought all the land of Egypt for Pharaoh; for the Egyptians sold every man his field, because the famine prevailed over them: so the land became Pharaoh's"* (v. 20).

The people didn't sow—Joseph sowed. The people spent while Joseph stored. Joseph became the *"boss"* in this recession. In the famine, he was the only one with food. When the people came to him for grain, they paid with their money. When their money was exhausted, they paid with livestock and lands! All the land in Egypt became Pharaoh's because one man believed, obeyed, and sowed seed. The money was always there, but it was only transferred when Joseph followed the three-step process. Joseph's wealth was sitting in Egypt and in Canaan all the time.

We must understand that every time a wealth transfer occurred in a famine or recession, the wealth was already there waiting. Major wealth transfers almost always occur during times of recession. Stop looking at a recession as something negative. Turn it around for your good by viewing it from the right perspective. God expects you to think differently than the world. Are you going to be the boss or the servant in this recession?

Israel Experienced Famine

The Israelites had been slaves for 400 years in Egypt. They had been in bondage. God was ready to deliver them from their recession. Initially, the Hebrews believed the Word of God. God told them to take the wealth from the Egyptians before they departed the land.

Exodus 12:35 says, *"And the children of Israel did according to the word of Moses; and they borrowed of the Egyptians jewels of silver, and jewels of gold, and raiment."*

Now the King James translation says they "borrowed" from the Egyptians, but the word "borrow" implies that you are using something that belongs to another and you are going to give it back. A better word would be that they "spoiled" the Egyptians. The Children of Israel had absolutely no intention of giving anything back. They took gold, silver, and the wealth of the Egyptians.

> **The Children of Israel took gold, silver, and the wealth of the Egyptians.**

The children of Israel had been in a different kind of famine—a famine of freedom. Their ancestors had sold themselves as servants, and they had to build Pharaoh's buildings. They were slaves of Pharaoh, they ate only what they were told to eat, and they worked eighteen to twenty hours a day for their food. Now that's a recession!

But in *Exodus 12:35,* we read that the Israelites spoiled the Egyptians of their silver, gold, and their finest clothing as they left under Moses. They were heading out for the Promised Land, but God did not want them leaving the land broke. He wanted them loaded! Former slaves were now asking their former masters for their stuff! God caused them to have favor to get whatever they asked for. They stripped the Egyptians of their wealth.

But they really were not taking the wealth of Egypt. They were taking back God's wealth. Why? How did the wealth get to Egypt? A man of God by the name of Joseph had a plan from God, and when he obeyed the plan of God, the wealth showed up in Egypt. Joseph had brought that wealth to Egypt in the first place by following the voice of God. The Israelites were just gathering up what already belonged to the Lord before heading out of town. And now God's people were leaving, and they were taking all the wealth with them. This was God's wealth. They spoiled the plague-ravaged Egyptians, and the Egyptians could do nothing about it.

Exodus 12:36 says, *"And the Lord gave the people favour in the sight of the Egyptians, so that they lent unto them such things as they required. And they spoiled the Egyptians."*

But the Children of Israel had no idea that the gold and the silver wasn't their harvest. After God led them out, the Israelites asked, "Why did God bring us out into the desert?" Most couldn't look past the desert and the apparent lack. But they were on *their way* to their blessing.

While they were in the desert, they assumed all that wealth was theirs. In a recession, we have to beware of settling for less than what God has for us. God does not want you to barely get by. He wants you to prosper. They had to believe God would take care of them. If they really believed, they would obey God.

The *Promised Land* was their harvest. The blessing was in the houses they didn't build, the furniture they didn't buy, the sheep they didn't raise, the fruit trees they didn't plant—those things made up their harvest, their blessing.

In *Joshua 1:3* we read, *"Every place that the sole of your foot shall tread upon, that have I given unto you, as I said unto Moses."* "Have I given" is past tense. The only thing they had to do was walk.

Your blessings are already here. Your abundance is already here. God isn't going to command it. There's no FedEx service coming from heaven. Everything you need is sitting on planet earth. Who has it? Someone, like the Philistines, has your house. Someone has your lands. Someone has your car. Someone has things that belong to you. The moment you obey God, it is going to come to you. But if you don't obey God, it isn't going to come. Your obedience has to be by faith; without faith you can't please God (*Hebrews 11:6*). Without faith He can't operate on your behalf.

God said, "The moment you put your foot on the Promised Land, it's yours." But the Israelites allowed fear to take them on a journey of forty years that could have been done in forty days.

Wherever Your Feet Tread

"There are giants in the land," most of the spies sent into the Promised Land complained. That should not have had anything to do with it. God said, "Everywhere you put your foot, it's yours." God said, "So what about the giants? They have nothing to do with it. I have already given the land to you."

He's saying the same today: "The giants of fear are actually living in your house and driving your car. They actually own your property. I have already given it to you, but because of disobedience you will not be able to see it."

Those Israelites never put their feet on the Promised Land. If they had, that very moment it would have been theirs. God was going to be their protection. But they thought the silver and the gold was their harvest, and they listened to reports of fear instead of God's instructions. The silver and gold was not their harvest, so why did God make them take it?

Exodus 25:1-2 say, *"And the LORD spake unto Moses, saying, Speak unto the children of Israel, that they bring me an offering."* You may be wondering, "Are you telling me that God is commanding an offering?" Yes, this was God. Why? Because blessing follows a seed. The Promised Land could never have come without an offering.

God goes on to say He wanted offerings from those who were willing to give from the heart, but He's saying, "Tell them not to just tip Me. Tell them not to give Me the leftovers. Tell them not to look in their wallet and find the smallest bill they can.

The next verses tell us what kind of offering He wanted:

And this is the offering which ye shall take of them; gold, and silver, and brass, and blue, and purple, and scarlet, and fine linen, and goats' hair, and rams' skins dyed red, and badgers' skins, and shittim wood, oil for the light, spices for anointing oil, and for sweet incense, onyx stones, and stones to be set in the ephod, and in the breastplate.

(Exodus 25:3-7)

> **God is saying, "I want the things you thought were your blessing. It's not your blessing. It's the seed."**

They gave Him the best, the best of what they had spoiled from the Egyptians. If you wish to be blessed by God, you can't just tip God. No more giving Him the equivalent of blemished animals and financial leftovers—not if you want to walk in the blessing.

God was saying, "I want the things you thought were your blessing. It's not your blessing. It's the seed."

"The seed for what?" they could have asked.

And God would have answered, "The seed for the Promised Land—a land filled with milk and honey, with animals you didn't have to tend and houses you didn't have to build."

Every time you give seed into God's Kingdom, it is for God's work just like theirs was.

Why did the Lord want all this stuff? *"And let them make Me a sanctuary; that I may dwell among them"* (v. 8). Could the Israelites ever have gotten to the Promised Land without the right seed? No, not at all. The spoils from Egypt was the seed that gave them the houses they didn't build, the furniture they didn't buy, fruit trees they didn't plant, and herds and flocks they didn't raise.

Why did they wait 40 years? Remember those three keys to blessing I told you about? **Obey the voice of God, believe the Word, and sow the seed.** They only got two out of three. Which one was missing? They obeyed the voice and they sowed the seed, but they didn't believe the Word. Instead of moving into the Promised Land, they allowed fear to keep them in the desert for 40 years (*Hebrews 4:1*). They didn't believe God's Word that had said, "I have **given** you everywhere your foot will tread."

That's why the Bible says they never entered the Promised Land—they never entered God's rest. They thought they had to fight the giants, yet God had never told them to fight the giants. He had said, "Wherever your foot treads, it's yours!"

Hebrews 4:1 says the Children of Israel had their chance to enter the Promised Land as God had intended—an offer to enter His rest that endures to us today. But the word they had heard was not mixed with faith.

They did not trust that the land was already theirs to take. They were intimidated by the giants in the land, and thought they would be incapable of fighting against them. They believed the battle was theirs to fight. They missed the Promised Land because they did not mix their seed with faith. You must believe, obey, and sow your seed before you can obtain a blessing transfer.

The Israelites didn't see things from God's perspective. Those people who occupied the Promised Land were only there to build the houses, raise the flocks, and plant the vineyards for the Children of Israel. But their lease was up in Canaan, and they were about to be evicted by God. Everything was ripe and ready for the Israelites to show up and walk on it. It was all in place, but because they did not mix their seed with faith, that generation never saw any of it. The word God had spoken was, "I have given you the land." That was already a done deal.

It makes me wonder what would have happened if they had simply obeyed.

The Word shows us many people who did obey, however, and walked in God's blessing. As we read these examples, I hope you let them sink in, for their circumstances were not easy, either. They lived in times of lack, and their obedience required tremendous faith, as yours does today.

Chapter 10
Elijah Spreads the Blessing

That generation of the Children of Israel did not meet God's requirements. They allowed fear—fear of the giants in the land—to keep them from the Promised Land. But other stories in the Bible recount great acts of obedience by ordinary, fallible people just like you and me.

Let's look at Elijah's story in *1 Kings 17*. Here we will see God moving, touching His people, changing His people, and blessing His people in the middle of a famine.

First Kings 17:1 says, *"And Elijah the Tishbite, who was of the inhabitants of Gilead, said unto Ahab, As the LORD God of Israel liveth, before whom I stand, there shall not be dew nor rain these years, but according to my word."*

No rain meant a famine was coming—no rain meant no crops; no crops meant nothing to eat. The Lord kept the rain from coming for three and one-half years.

We know it took three and one-half years because when James talks about the fervent prayer of a righteous man that avails much in *James 5:16*, he then says, *"Elijah was a man with a nature like ours, and he prayed earnestly that it would not rain; and it did not rain on the land for three years and six months"* (v. 17). That's what the fervent prayer of a righteous man will do.

Did Elijah want to go through the famine? No! Elijah said, "Lord, what about me? I don't want to go through a famine." God said, "No problem. This famine is no surprise. I already have you covered."

"What am I to do?" Elijah prayed. And God gave him direction. *First Kings 17:2* says, *"Then the word of the LORD came to him."* Remember, God always gives instruction. He gives you a seed, and He gives you instruction. He always meets your need through a seed.

In the verses that follow, God gives Elijah an instruction, but I want to digress for a moment. God spoke direction into Elijah's life so that he would not be affected by the recession. You will need to *seek* God for what to do in any recession.

Seeking God

In the middle of a recession, we had better learn to call on Him. Every instruction requires obedience. If you do not call on Him, you will never get the instruction. The first step is to call on the Lord.

Jeremiah 33:1-3 says,

Moreover, the word of the Lord came to Jeremiah the second time, while he was still shut up in the court of the guard, saying, Thus says the Lord Who made [the earth], the Lord Who formed it to establish it—the Lord is His name: Call to Me and I will answer you and show you great and mighty things, fenced in and hidden, which you do not know (do not distinguish and recognize, have knowledge of and understand).

(AMP)

Answers do not come until somebody calls. **God speaks little, but answers much.** God will talk to you when you do some calling. He always answers. He cannot reply when no request has been made.

> **God speaks little, but answers much.**

God does not stress out over any recession. This is not a hard thing for God to fix. *Jeremiah 32:27* says, *"Behold, I am the Lord, the God of all flesh; is there anything too hard for Me?"* (AMP)

Jeremiah 29:11 says, *"For I know the thoughts and plans that I have for you, says the Lord, thoughts and plans for welfare and peace and not for evil, to give you hope in your final outcome"* (AMP).

God has a plan for your prosperity in the middle of any recession. You have to believe His plan. If you do not believe His plan, you will remove yourself from His best. When you do not believe, you miss the first key to prospering in a recession. You cannot proceed to step two if you do not fulfill step one.

Christians often waste seed by just throwing something into the offering bucket. Seed is wasted when you do your own thing rather than ask for instructions. When you know the right seed to sow and then obey, you will see your harvest. The wrong seed is wasted seed. Seed is wasted every Sunday in churches all over the world.

People don't ask God first for an instruction. From this point on, do not waste your precious seed by neglecting to seek God before you give. Pray and obey. Whatever God instructs is the right seed; whatever you determine is wasted seed. God's plan is always there, but it is our job to find out what that plan is.

When you call, God hears and answers. *Jeremiah 29:12-14* says, *"Then you will call upon Me and go and pray to Me, and I will listen to you. And you will seek Me and find Me, when you search for Me with all your heart. I will be found by you, says the LORD."*

The only reason God does not speak to people is that they never call upon Him. Your part is to call, and His part is to answer. When you seek God with all your heart, you will find Him. He is not playing hide-and-seek. He always responds to the calls of His children. But you first have to do some seeking if you ever expect to find. God promises that you will find Him when you seek. We have to take God at His Word and call upon Him. Elijah called upon the Lord, and God responded with an instruction.

In *1 Kings 17:3-4* God says, *"Get away from here and turn eastward, and hide by the Brook Cherith, which flows into the Jordan. And it will be that you shall drink from the brook, and I have commanded the ravens to feed you there."*

That means there was a brook called Cherith waiting for someone to drink from it and a bunch of ravens flying around with meat and bread with no one to give it to.

> **God has already commanded your provision, abundance, and blessing in this recession, but you will never see it without obedience.**

God has already commanded your provision, abundance, and blessing in this recession, but you will never see it without obedience.

Elijah, a man like us, needed only to speak a word at God's direction, and it stopped raining for three and one-half years.

But even that mighty man of God had to follow directions. He could have complained and asked, "I don't want to go to Cherith. Can't You have the ravens come to me? Can't You find a brook that's closer?"

Your provision is on the other side of your obedience. Had Elijah gone to any other brook, he would have missed his provision. So what did he do? He obeyed the Word of God.

In this time, just as in Elijah's time, it is critical that you obey God's Word and His voice!

People come to me all the time and say, "Why do bad things happen to good people?" Usually, it's because they don't obey. God always knows when recessions are coming long before they ever show up, and He has already made a way out of each one of them. But we are going to have to pray and obey.

Elijah's provision was already in the right place. Your provision is always in the right place. Recessions are never a shock to God.

We read that Elijah did indeed obey: *"So he went and did according unto the word of the LORD: for he went and dwelt by the brook Cherith, that is before Jordan. And the ravens brought him bread and flesh in the morning, bread and flesh in the evening; and he drank of the brook"* *(1 Kings 17:5-6).*

Isn't it interesting that the ravens, who were scavengers, didn't eat the meat? And they obviously didn't bake the bread. He's in a recession, yet Elijah is eating steak and bread in the morning and evening, and he's drinking all the fresh water he desires. He's doing really well for being in the middle of a famine!

Don't tell me you are supposed to participate in a recession. God is already taking care of you. Your blessing is on the other side of your obedience.

But what about the rain and the end of the recession? We're getting to that: *"And it came to pass after a while, that the brook dried up, because there had been no rain in the land"* (v. 7). Was this a shock to God? Did God say, "Oh, my goodness! I wasn't planning on this. The recession is really getting serious! What am I going to do with My people"? No, He has already made a way out.

Elijah probably got on his knees and prayed, "Lord, I know that this recession is no surprise to You. What do I do now? You said You would never leave me or forsake me. You said you would take care of me, be with me, and provide all my needs. What do You want me to do?"

He Will Answer You

How do you know God will give you direction? Does the Bible say, "Call on Me and I will avoid you"? No! It says, *"He shall call upon Me, and I will answer him; I will be with him in trouble; I will deliver him and honor him"* (Psalm 91:15). The Bible says, *"However, when He, the Spirit of truth, has come, He will guide you into all truth; for He will not speak on His own authority, but whatever He hears He will speak; and He will tell you things to come"* (John 16:13).

Let's look at *1 Kings 17:8-9* and God's next instruction: *"Then the word of the LORD came to him, saying, 'Arise, go to Zarephath, which belongs to Sidon, and dwell there. See, I have commanded a widow there to provide for you.'"*

His provision **was commanded**—that's past tense! God has already commanded your provision as well. **Provision is always waiting on the other side of your obedience.** Always! Always! Always!

> Provision is always waiting on the other side of your obedience.

So was God testing Elijah, just to see if he'd jump? No—the provision was right where He said it was. It says, *"So he arose and went to Zarephath. And when he came to the gate of the city, indeed a widow was there gathering sticks. And he called to her and said, 'Please bring me a little water in a cup, that I may drink'"* (v. 10).

Water was expensive. Why? No rain. Yet Elijah said, "I want some water." He had walked six days to get there, so he was probably thirsty. Verse 11 says, *"And as she was going to get it, he called to her and said, 'Please bring me a morsel of bread in your hand.'"*

God had already spoken to this widow woman, and said, "Feed My man." She should have been looking for him. She was not in obedience, and the famine came. When she lost her house, she prayed. No answer. She lost her furniture and prayed. No answer. Finally, she lost all of her savings and prayed. No answer. Why was there no answer to her prayers? She was in direct disobedience.

Blessings do not come to the disobedient. How do we know she was in disobedience? Because God told Elijah that he had "commanded." That is past tense. God told her, "Go find My man," but she didn't obey, and now she's down to her last meal. She had lost it all.

Look at *1 Kings 17:12* which says, *"So she said, 'As the LORD your God lives, I do not have bread, only a handful of flour in a bin, and a little oil in a jar; and see, I am gathering a couple of sticks that I may go in and prepare it for myself and my son, that we may eat it, and die.'"*

She was saying, "All I've got left is for one adult and one child. We're going to eat our last meal, and then we'll starve."

Does dying of starvation come easier on a full stomach? **The widow was looking at what little she had left as her harvest. But Elijah was looking at what she had left as a seed.**

What causes the seed to multiply? The anointing. And when the anointing hit, that seed had to multiply. Elijah was going to cause this seed to grow. How was he going to do that? It says, *"And Elijah said to her, 'Do not fear; go and do as you have said, but make me a small cake from it first, and bring it to me; and afterward make some for yourself and your son'"* (v. 13).

In other words, he was telling her to put God's work before her own. That's why Elijah said, "Feed me first." Because the day you do that—put God first—the anointing is going to get on your seed and cause it to explode.

Elijah told her, *"For thus says the LORD God of Israel: 'The bin of flour shall not be used up, nor shall the jar of oil run dry, until the day the LORD sends rain on the earth'"* (v. 14). The drought lasted three and one-half years!

The Lord was telling her that if she obeyed, she wouldn't exhaust His provision by feeding His prophet first. Whatever she had left, God guaranteed it would be there tomorrow. God promised that whatever she used He would replace with more the next day.

Elijah spoke to that seed and the anointing on God's Word caused it to grow. In *1 Kings 17:15-16*, we read about the results:

So she went away and did according to the word of Elijah; and she and he and her household ate for many days. The bin of flour was not used up, nor did the jar of oil run dry, according to the word of the LORD which He spoke by Elijah.

Back in verse 12, it was the widow woman and her son who were going to eat and die. By faith she made that little meal and fed the man of God, herself, and the boy. Yet there was so much left over that she sold it on the streets. She got all of her servants back, and now she has a *household*.

The next day she woke up. She had a little meal and little oil. By faith, she made it up again and fed the man of God, herself, her son, and the servants. And again, she had some left over. She got all of her furniture back.

The next day she woke up, and she had a little meal and little oil. That's all there was. She had to prepare the food every day *by faith*. It fed Elijah, herself, her son, and all the servants. There was enough left over, so she sold it on the streets. She bought a two-story house and gave Elijah the upstairs guest room. Now that's pretty good for a widow who was preparing to die.

It took the believed Word for the widow woman to say, "I'll do it. I'll take whatever I have left, my last meal, and I'll put God first. I will obey you."

She obeyed the voice of God through the prophet and gave her seed, believing in faith that God would do as He said He would— even in the middle of a devastating recession.

Of course, God did exactly that—He blessed her in the middle of that recession.

Chapter 11
Blessed Man of God

In *2 Kings 3:16,* yet another recession is going on. Again, there's no water. The Lord gave instruction through the prophet Elisha: *"Thus saith the LORD, Make this valley full of ditches."* "What in the world are we going to do with ditches?" King Jehoshaphat might have asked.

Dry ditches may not seem like provision during a drought, but you'd better obey God.

Elisha goes on, *"For thus saith the LORD, Ye shall not see wind, neither shall ye see rain; yet that valley shall be filled with water, that ye may drink, both ye, and your cattle, and your beasts"* (v. 17).

Sounds like God is about to do a miracle. He is about to give everything needed in the middle of a recession. Verse 18 says, *"And this is a simple matter in the sight of the LORD."* God blessing you in the midst of a recession is a *simple* thing—it's easy for Him!

When you know your God, recession isn't a big deal. I'm expecting some major provision, because the world is going to let it go, and it is going to come to those who obey God's Word. I'm going to obey the Lord, and I'm going to be a blessing to those around me, spreading the Good News of the Gospel.

It is a simple matter for God to take care of me and my family, and it's just as simple for Him to take care of you!

Elisha continues to prophesy to the gathered kings, *"He will also deliver the Moabites into your hand. Also you shall attack every fortified city and every choice city"* (v. 18-19). In other words, God told them they'd have victory over their enemies and enjoy victory wherever they went.

But what about the seed? Let's read on.

Verse 20 says, *"And it came to pass in the morning, when the meat offering was offered, that, behold, there came water by the way of Edom, and the country was filled with water."* The water didn't actually show up until the seed was planted—until they offered up their offering.

Notice also that the water was already in Edom waiting to gush into those trenches. That water did not come from heaven! It was already here on the earth. Likewise, the things that God wants to transfer to you are already on the earth.

So these kings approached Elisha for the Word of the Lord, and they obeyed by digging seemingly-worthless holes in the ground and offering their seed. And God responded with the provision of water, despite the drought. Not only that, if we read on, we would see that God used that blessing—the water—to confuse the Moabites. God made the water look like blood. The Moabites thought they had destroyed each other. When the Moabites rushed to collect the spoils, they found the armies waiting for them.

The Israelites did indeed rout Moab and chase them back into their towns, defeating them as they went, just as God said they would.

The Lord has provision waiting for you, even—and perhaps especially—when obeying doesn't seem to make sense to you. God says "Put Me first," as He asks for the little you have remaining. "Go dig dry holes in the heat of the day," might sound like an onerous, cruel chore, but you'd better obey God.

You must never forget that, no matter how foolish it may seem, your provision is on the other side of your obedience. Obey the voice of the Lord.

> **Digging holes might sound like a cruel chore, but if God tells you to dig, you better obey!**

Oil Overflow

So we have read about a widow who gave away her last meal and kings who dug dry ditches; but God provided and blessed them—blessing made possible because of their obedience to His voice.

Let's go on and look at another example of His provision during recession, not in a country-wide famine this time, but in one woman's personal life. Elisha had a group of prophets that he worked with, and after one of them died, his widow came to Elisha with a problem. *Second Kings 4:1* says,

A certain woman of the wives of the sons of the prophets cried out to Elisha, saying, 'Your servant my husband is dead, and you know that your servant feared the LORD. And the creditor is coming to take my two sons to be his slaves.'

This woman's personal recession was so bad her sons were about to be taken into slavery—and in that era, those boys would be responsible for caring for their widowed mother. This is a serious recession; her husband is dead, and her future is about to be carried away.

You may have lost your house or your car, but wait a minute. Have you lost any kids yet? She's about to lose her kids. This is how serious this thing was.

She went to the man of God for help. *"So Elisha said to her, 'What shall I do for you? Tell me, what do you have in the house?'"* (v. 2). He knew how God worked—he'd followed Elijah around and learned God's ways. By this time, he had been the man of God for years and he knew that in order to provide a blessing, God needed a seed. Elisha was saying, "God will multiply and bring a blessing, but I need a seed. A hundred times zero is still zero. Give me a seed."

She answered, *"Your maidservant has nothing in the house but a jar of oil" (2 Kings 4:2)*. She was broke. I mean, can you imagine when the only thing you've got in your house is a jar of olive oil?

Elisha didn't see that bottle of oil as her harvest. He saw it as seed God was about to multiply.

In her mind she thought this was nothing, because she saw the jar of oil as her harvest. Elisha didn't see that bottle of oil as her harvest. He saw it as seed that God was about to multiply.

Now, would she obey the Word of the Lord? Let's find out.

Elisha told her exactly what to do: *"Then he said, 'Go, borrow vessels from everywhere, from all your neighbors—empty vessels; do not gather just a few"* (v. 3).

Miracles are about to happen!

In *2 Kings 4:4*, Elisha said, *"And when you have come in, you shall shut the door behind you and your sons; then pour it into all those vessels, and set aside the full ones."*

Notice, God gave her an instruction through Elisha. Elisha could have paid her debt, but he didn't. God didn't tell him to pay her debt, but God told him to give her an instruction. I have said it before, but it is worth repeating: **the instruction you obey is the future you create.** Just obey, because in doing so, you are going to release the anointing on your seed.

Look at what happened: *"So she went from him and shut the door behind her and her sons, who brought the vessels to her; and she poured it out"* (v. 5).

In other words, she was a doer of the Word. She obeyed the instruction. It didn't make any sense, but she did it. And here's what God did: *"Now it came to pass, when the vessels were full, that she said to her son, 'Bring me another vessel.' And he said to her, 'There is not another vessel.' So the oil ceased"* (v. 6).

She should have gone into the vessel-making business! What if she had hundreds of them, or thousands? How much oil would she have had then?

As she began to pour that little jar of oil into the first vessel, she probably felt a little silly. This did not make any sense in the natural. But then she poured and poured, filling all the vessels she had borrowed. Once the vessels ran out, so did the oil. It was the vessels that ran out first—not the oil.

The harvest is always limited by the vessels. So if she only believed God for three vessels and that's where her faith was, she would have received three. If she had faith for thirty vessels, then she would have had thirty.

The anointing is limited to your faith level. Had she borrowed more vessels, the anointing would have been sustained until all the vessels were full. She would have been the first olive oil magnate, the Sheik of the East, an oil baroness. She only needed enough money to get out of debt, but that is not what set the limit on her blessing.

> **Your level of faith is based on the Word you have believed.**

Your level of faith is based on the Word you have believed.

I imagine she was very excited by all of this, and she went to tell Elisha what had happened. It says, *"Then she came and told the man of God. And he said, 'Go, sell the oil and pay your debt; and you and your sons live on the rest'" (2 Kings 4:7).*

This woman's debt was her recession. She was about to lose her kids. But remember, God is able to do over and above and beyond whatever you can dream, think, or ask! *(Ephesians 3:20)* Not only was He concerned about getting her debt paid off, even more provision came because she planted the right seed. She was able to keep her kids and had a wagonload of money besides. Why? Because she was willing to obey.

Sacrificial Seed

When you read the Old Testament, it is important you read it with New Testament eyes. They didn't have the Bible as we know it to refer to, and they didn't have Jesus or the Holy Spirit living in them. They wrote things down the way they understood them. If you don't read the Old Testament with New Testament eyes, you can get a wrong impression about some passages.

We have talked about how obedience opens the doors to blessing, but it's also important to show that disobedience opens doors as well. Our sins have definite consequences, and when we reject God's ways and disobey, we open ourselves to the natural consequences of our actions.

Does God send pestilences and plagues on His people? I don't believe He does. However, when we sin, we sometimes reap from the seeds we've sown just as we reap from the godly seeds we've sown.

In *2 Samuel 24* we read of an instance where David's disobedience placed him and all of Israel in great jeopardy. It says, *"So the Lord sent a pestilence upon Israel."* God is a good God, and He doesn't send recession! But when these people saw the pestilence, all they could see was, "God must have sent it." What was this pestilence? It was a plague that killed people, and David's disobedience had opened the door to it. The Bible tells us, *"And there died of the people from Dan even to Beersheba seventy thousand men"* (v. 15).

Verse 17 says: *"And David spake unto the LORD when he saw the angel that smote the people, and said, Lo, I have sinned, and I have done wickedly: but these sheep, what have they done? let thine hand, I pray thee, be against me, and against my father's house."*

It's interesting to note that David's prayers did not stop the plague, but his prayers brought an instruction. God didn't meet his need, but He did give David an opportunity to obey.

> **David's prayers did not stop the plague, but his prayers brought an instruction.**

God did not speak to David at this point, but He did speak to the prophet Gad. It says, *"And Gad came that day to David, and said unto him, Go up, rear an altar unto the LORD in the threshing floor of Araunah the Jebusite. And David, according to the saying of Gad, went up as the LORD commanded"* (v. 18-19).

The Lord **commanded an offering**. There was the believed Word, the voice of God. Now let's look for the seed.

> *Now Araunah looked, and saw the king and his servants coming toward him. So Araunah went out and bowed before the king with his face to the ground. Then Araunah said, 'Why has my lord the king come to his servant?' And David said, 'To buy the threshing floor from you, to build an altar to the LORD, that the plague may be withdrawn from the people.'*
> *(2 Samuel 24:20-21)*

God told David to build an altar on Araunah's threshing floor, and David is about to have another opportunity to obey...or not.

Now Araunah said to David, 'Let my lord the king take and offer up whatever seems good to him. Look, here are oxen for burnt sacrifice, and threshing implements and the yokes of the oxen for wood. All these, O king, Araunah has given to the king.' And Araunah said to the king, 'May the LORD your God accept you.'
(v. 22-23)

Araunah, being loyal to David and desiring to honor God, offers David what seems like a great opportunity—offer the sacrifice, at no *cost* to him. Araunah offers to pick up the tab, so to speak. This is David's opportunity *not* to obey; it's his chance to take God's instructions and twist them just a little to his advantage. If he does, he will be missing the significance of a sacrifice, which is the sowing of a seed.

Let's read the next verse and see what David, a man after God's own heart, does.

Then the king said to Araunah, 'No, but I will surely buy it from you for a price; nor will I offer burnt offerings to the LORD my God with that which costs me nothing.' So David bought the threshing floor and the oxen for fifty shekels of silver.
(2 Samuel 24:24)

The king said, "No deal, guy. I cannot take your oxen. I will never give God something that doesn't have value to me. I will never give God something that doesn't have worth to me. If it isn't valuable to me, it's not valuable to God."

I asked the Lord one day, "Lord, what is this deal about it costing David? Do You really care?" He said, "I'm not really interested in the sheep, and I wasn't really interested in the offering."

I said, "Lord, why do You keep asking for offerings? You don't want them. You don't need them, so why do You take them from us?"

> **Your offering is the only visible evidence of your faith.**

He said, "You don't understand, son. *Your offering is the only visible evidence of your faith.*" If you say by faith, "God, I'm believing You for big things," God could respond, "Then, where is the evidence?" That's why Jesus said that the woman who put in the two mites put in more than all the others *(Mark 12:43)*. He was looking at what she had left. In other words, He was measuring her faith.

God is not trying to take your money. He is measuring your faith. He was never interested in your money. Every time we give an offering, it never goes to heaven.

So why would He tell you to sow something you weren't planning to sow? Why do you have to give Him something that costs you something? Because now your faith is attached to it. That's the believed Word.

"So David bought the threshing floor and the oxen for fifty shekels of silver" (v. 24). Fifty shekels of silver would be a lot of money back then. Remember, David could have got it for free, but he said, "No, I'm not going to do that. I'm not going to give God something that costs me nothing." If it means nothing to you, it means nothing to God. It's the evidence of your trust in Him. If you trust Him with little, He won't trust you with much.

If we are going to walk in the fullness of the blessing—if we're going to walk in the *extravagant* blessing in the midst of a recession—we have to get this thing right. Every time it is offering time, do two things: pray and obey. Whatever God tells you, obey!

God's not trying to get anything from you, because there is nothing you have that He needs. He is trying to get something *to*

The wrong seed has never been able to bring the right harvest.

you. The wrong seed has never been able to bring the right harvest.

Let me say it another way; had David taken this man's oxen for free, the plague would not have stopped. In our next chapter we will further explore the subject of sacrifice and seed. There is a powerful principle within this subject that I know you will want to apply in your life.

Chapter 12
The Cost of Sacrificial Seed

In the previous chapter, we read about David's disobedience and his opportunity to set things right with a sacrifice. But we also saw that he had a chance to make an offering to the Lord that didn't cost him anything.

We recognized that David, a man after God's own heart, understood that the value of a sacrifice comes from the value that he placed on it. Because it cost him something—it was truly a sacrifice!

"David built there an altar unto the LORD, and offered burnt offerings and peace offerings" (2 Samuel 24:25). It cost him fifty shekels of silver. As far as God was concerned, this was fifty shekels worth of faith. What happened when there was fifty shekels worth of faith? *"So the LORD heeded the prayers for the land, and the plague was withdrawn from Israel" (v. 25)*.

When you give your seed, you must make sure it means something to you. You can follow the Holy Spirit, you can believe the Word, but if you neglect the seed—the sacrifice—you can limit the blessing.

> **When you give your seed, you must make sure it means something to you.**

You might say, "I can give God anything I want."

Really? Let's read *Malachi 1:9*, which says, *"But now entreat God's favor, that He may be gracious to us. While this is being done by your hands, will He accept you favorably?"* What does this mean?

Let's look at verses 9-10 from *The Amplified*:

Now then, I [Malachi] beg [you priests], entreat God [earnestly] that He will be gracious to us. With such a gift from your hand [as a defective animal for sacrifice], will He accept it or show favor to any of you? says the Lord of hosts. Oh, that there were even one among you [whose duty it is to minister to Me] who would shut the doors, that you might not kindle fire on My altar to no purpose [an empty, futile, fruitless pretense]! I have no pleasure in you, says the Lord of hosts, nor will I accept an offering from your hand.

This is heavy. Why did God say this? Because they were bringing defective, blemished animals, and God said, "I am tired of you giving Me your leftovers, because there is no faith in that. You show me your faith when you give something that has value to you."

David could have accepted the offer of a *free* sacrifice, and offered that to God as an easy way out. He could have seen *that* as his blessing. But that wasn't what God had said—He had told David to sacrifice to Him there, and David knew how sowing seed worked with God. It had to be a *real* sacrifice.

God's provision for us in a time of recession is always available. His hand is always poised to bless us. But you must realize that it works in a particular way, and the seed we sow must be sacrificial seed.

Sow Your Seed Even During Famines

Remember our keys to blessing—the Word believed, obey the Holy Spirit, and sowing your seed. And as we've been seeing in the life of David, there is no such thing as an easy sacrifice. It has to have meaning and value.

> **There is no such thing as an easy sacrifice.**

Abram followed God's instruction, and he was willing to sow a very precious seed—Sarai, his wife. And God used that opportunity to send Abram away from Egypt loaded. Abram believed the Word, obeyed the Spirit, and the seed showed up.

Joseph knew famine as well, but God's favor elevated Joseph out of prison and put him in a position to not only save lives—including those of his family—but to show God's greatness to His people years later. Joseph's blessing extended onto Pharaoh's business and harvests, and the very wealth that people traded for the stores of food was the very wealth the Children of Israel carried away from Egypt. The blessing follows a seed, and the wealth with which they left was later the seed sown as an offering for entry to the Promised Land.

We learn a lesson from those Israelites—do not confuse your seed with your blessing. An entire generation of them learned it the hard way, dying in the wilderness on a journey that should have taken a little over a month. They only understood two of the three keys. Remember, they obeyed the voice of God and they had a seed, but they didn't believe God's Word when He told them that they would take the land.

The widow that Elijah ministered to could have seen her little remaining reserves as her blessing, but she obeyed and made food for the prophet. She put God first, before herself and her son, and she watched as the store of food stretched on and on and on! This was because of the anointing Elijah passed on to it.

King Jehoshaphat believed Elisha and had ditches dug in a dry valley. But it was only after the morning offering, when that seed was sown, that water came and filled those ditches.

The widow, whose husband died in service to Elisha, was in a desperate situation with her creditor coming to take her sons. The prophet of God knew how God worked. He knew that she would have to obey an instruction and sow a seed. When she did, the oil started to flow and the only thing that stopped it was her ability to gather vessels. She could have gone into the oil business if she had more vessels. But God met her need according to her seed.

What Is Your Seed?

When we see the reports of recession and financial famines we now know we should do the opposite of what the world is doing. Now it is time to sow seed!

You may say, "Brother Nasir, what do I need to sow? How much do I sow?" I have no idea, and it's not my business. That's between you and God. But be assured of this; God will direct you and tell you what to sow.

God's Word also says, *"So let each one give as he purposes in his heart, not grudgingly or of necessity; for God loves a cheerful giver"* *(2 Corinthians 9:7).*

At offering time, we should give from our heart, not reluctantly or in response to pressure.

Have you been walking in recession instead of blessing? Have you been listening to the fear the media spouts and putting your wallet away when you have the chance to sow seed? Maybe you've been "tipping" God and giving Him your leftovers?

Some of the very ones who do this are those who cry the loudest and get mad at God because of recession in their lives.

God has a way out of recession for you and me, but it requires something of us. It requires praying and asking Him to instruct us. It requires obedience when He gives that instruction. And it requires a seed that is truly a sacrifice to us, something that has worth and value.

If you feel that recession and plagues have been overcoming you, it is time to ask yourself if you have been failing to do these things. It's time to examine the seed you sow, because the wrong seed will never reap the right harvest.

A few dollars thrown in the offering bucket isn't going to reap the harvest of blessings that God wants to bless you with during a recession. Your leftovers or blemished, grudging sacrifice won't cut it!

When God gives you instruction regarding the seed you are to sow, you must sow that and exactly that—nothing more and nothing less than what God instructs. You must sow the right seed, and then you will watch as God responds to that obedience.

The days of throwing your spare change in buckets are over. The days of letting someone else pay to spread the Gospel are over. The days of pushing aside God's voice telling you to give to someone else are over.

It's time for the right sacrifice, the right seed that releases the blessing He wants to give you.

If you want to walk in the fullness of God's blessing and prosper in the middle of a recession then you need to make this decision.

God loves a cheerful giver.	When it is time to give I will believe His Word, obey His voice and plant my seed *"not grudgingly, or of necessity; for God loveth a cheerful giver"* *(2 Corinthians 9:7).*

But why would Paul have to remind the Corinthians of this? For the answer, we must look at the church in Philippi.

Only the Philippians Listened

Philippians 4:19 says, *"And my God will liberally supply (fill to the full) your every need according to His riches in glory in Christ Jesus"* (AMP). Nowhere in this verse does it say your needs will only be met if there is not a recession. God is going to take care of all of your needs all of the time. Paul wrote this to the Philippian church, whose first pastor was an unemployed jailer.

The Philippian church got started when Paul and Silas went through Philippi and were imprisoned *(Acts 16:12-34).* But rather than complain, they chose to praise God in the middle of their recession. First they prayed for their release, and then they sang praises to God so loudly that the other prisoners heard them. As they praised God, the power of God hit the jail, and all the shackles fell off and the prison doors swung open.

The jailer was ready to kill himself thinking all the prisoners had escaped. Paul and Silas convinced him not to kill himself and he became saved, he and his entire household. So the Philippian jailer became the first Philippian pastor. But they had a problem—they needed some money! He started this church in faith. Surely, the same God who freed Paul and Silas could also set them free financially.

The Philippian church started off in recession, but they took the necessary steps to get in position for the blessing. In fact, the church became so wealthy that they were able to send men to travel with Paul in addition to meeting their own needs. This is what it means to have *an abundance for every good work.*

This was the only church that believed what Paul taught about giving. They obeyed the instruction by sowing into the work of God. The blessing continued to flow to them and through them—it wasn't a one-time offering.

Paul was excited about the harvest these Philippians were going to receive as a result of their faithful support. The Word of God says that when you sow, you will reap. The Thessalonians did not believe the Word. Had they believed, they would have sown when they were fed the Word. Rather than being doers of the Word, they held back. Those generous Philippians stepped in and took care of the tab (*Philippians 4:16-17*).

Paul says of their gift, *"Indeed I have all and abound. I am full, having received from Epaphroditus the things sent from you, a sweet-smelling aroma, an acceptable sacrifice, well pleasing to God"* *(Philippians 4:18).*

They sent funds over to Thessalonica to support Paul while he preached to the Thessalonian church. Those being fed should have been the ones sowing. Notice Paul never wrote this same message to the Thessalonians that God would supply all of their needs. They hadn't done their part to qualify.

Paul wrote his letter to the Philippians from Rome, where he arrived loaded after preaching the Gospel on the island of Malta. The Romans should have been taking care of Paul's needs, but again, they disqualified themselves from the blessing.

The Roman church also never received the same words Paul told the Philippians—that God would supply all their needs. The Philippians were the only ones who were giving into Paul's ministry, and they had sent over more gifts to Paul while he was in Rome. Their faithful giving caused their church to prosper.

The only church that believed, obeyed, and sowed the right seed was the crazy Philippian church. Consequently, they were the only ones who got the letter from Paul stating that God would supply all their needs in any recession. They would prosper regardless of the circumstances.

In *2 Corinthians 8:1-2,* we read Paul's testimony regarding the Philippians—that the churches of their area were blessed more than any others. They were full of joy, he writes in verse two, but they were also in the middle of recession. They were broke, but they refused to hold back. They just kept giving their way out of their recession. They were determined to give no matter what, and that is how they became prosperous when everyone else was struggling.

"For, as I can bear witness, [they gave] according to their ability, yes, and beyond their ability; and [they did it] voluntarily," Paul said of them in *2 Corinthians 8:3* (AMP).

In contrast, in *2 Corinthians 11:9* we read, *"And when I was with you and needed something, I was not a burden to anyone, for the brothers who came from Macedonia supplied what I needed. I have kept myself from being a burden to you in any way, and will continue to do so."*

Paul was ministering to the Corinthians, but they were not ministering to him. The Philippians were the Macedonians that Paul was referring to in this verse. They faithfully supported Paul's ministry. They had sent men to bring financial support to him in Corinth. They not only had plenty of finances to take care of things at their home church, but also enough to send helpers along with Paul as he traveled to other churches. When you can afford to do God's work full time and never have to worry about money, you have learned how to prosper in a recession. The Philippians operated in the blessing because they followed the three critical keys to success: believe, obey, and sow the right seed.

If you study both of the Corinthian letters, you will find out they were actually written in response to questions the Corinthians had regarding a financial recession they were experiencing. The content of Paul's letters indicates what the original letters were about. They wanted to know why they were not getting the jobs, the businesses, the bonuses, or the promotions. Everybody in the Corinthian church was struggling, and they wanted Paul's advice on what to do.

Paul gave an answer that revealed the root of the problem. He said they should not be unequally yoked. He was referring to Christian businessmen who had been in partnership with sinners. Those businesses were struggling because they were unequally yoked with the world.

Paul closed the letter with a powerful statement. He said he was to blame for the fact that they were struggling because he had failed to take up an offering after he taught them the Word. They had not been sowers.

Second Corinthians 12:13 says, *"For in what respect were you put to a disadvantage in comparison with the rest of the churches, unless [it was for the fact] that I myself did not burden you [with my financial support]? Pardon me [for doing you] this injustice!"* (AMP)

Paul did not make them sow, and as a result, they were in a recession. He closed the letter by saying, *"Pardon me for doing you this injustice."* Let that never be said of us! Instead, let us give the right seed at the right time and free up God's blessings!

The offerings that the Philippians sent to Paul were the right seed. Paul said it was an offering that God delighted in.

The Corinthians' Recession

The Corinthians had written to Paul regarding their recession. He wrote back to them and let them know of his plans to come to Corinth to minister to them. In *2 Corinthians 9:1*, he gave them advanced notice that he was going to take up an offering this time around.

He knew why they were struggling. The only way out of their trial was going to be the right seed. The Philippians were coming along with Paul, because they knew how to do this thing right.

Paul did not want to be embarrassed when he showed up and there was no offering prepared, so he was giving them advanced notice with his letter.

The Corinthian church wrote to Paul searching for a solution to their financial struggles. Paul was willing to come to them, but only on one condition. There was to be an offering already prepared. This was not just to be any ordinary offering, either. The offering was going to have to be bountiful. Paul knew they were struggling, but that was all the more reason to make this offering a big one! Paul was not asking for an offering because he wanted more stuff for his ministry. He had a different motive.

Second Corinthians 9:6 says, *"But this I say: He who sows sparingly will also reap sparingly, and he who sows bountifully will also reap bountifully."*

The only reason Paul asked for a bountiful offering was for their sakes, not his own purposes. He wanted to show them the only way out of their recession. If they sowed sparingly, they would only reap sparingly. They needed to sow a bountiful offering in this time of recession. The first element of the formula was that they needed to believe. The next step was the instruction. We find that in the next verse.

Second Corinthians 9:7 says,

Let each one [give] as he has made up his own mind and purposed in his heart, not reluctantly or sorrowfully or under compulsion, for God loves (He takes pleasure in, prizes above other things, and is unwilling to abandon or to do without) a cheerful (joyous, "prompt to do it") giver [whose heart is in his giving].

(AMP)

God lives in your heart. That is where He gives you the instruction. When it is offering time, do not look to your own understanding, but rather, go to your heart to hear what God will say. Obey what He tells you to do. God is not trying to get something from you. He always has a harvest in mind. You must believe God's motives are to bless you. If you believe that, you will seek God regarding the amount He wants you to give. Go to your heart and He will tell you what you should do.

Nowhere in this verse does it say this instruction does not pertain to times of recession. This applies even during a recession. This is the only way out of your recession.

In the next verse, *2 Corinthians 9:8* tells us what will happen if we do:

And God is able to make all grace (every favor and earthly blessing) come to you in abundance, so that you may always and un-

der all circumstances and whatever the need be self-sufficient
[possessing enough to require no aid or support and furnished
in abundance for every good work and charitable donation].
(AMP)

Grace is the anointing. You need God's favor in your marriage, with your children, in your health, in your finances, and in every area of your life. All grace is coming to those who obey. God will meet every need. Recessions will be powerless against you.

We are talking about abundant blessing here. The last thing on our minds right now should be how we are going to survive. With all the abundance that God gives you during a recession, you ought to be making plans about which good works you are going to support. Let's look at the next verse.

"As it is written, He [the benevolent person] scatters abroad; He gives to the poor; His deeds of justice and goodness and kindness and benevolence will go on and endure forever!" (2 Corinthians 9:9 AMP)

This verse is describing you—right in the middle of a recession! We are not just going to barely make it through. We are going to be the ones blessing the world. We will give to the poor. We will go out and do good works. Our own personal needs will have already been met. We will be releasing the blessing to people all around us. We are going to get the attention of the world. They will want to know this God who blesses people in the middle of a recession.

"And [God] Who provides seed for the sower and bread for eating will also provide and multiply your [resources for] sowing and increase the fruits of your righteousness [which manifests itself in active goodness, kindness, and charity]."
(2 Corinthians 9:10 AMP)

All your wealth has been down here on earth waiting for you. Your giving primes the pump of blessing and the flow is released. Businesses are going to explode. People are going to have favor in their places of employment. Promotions, bonuses, and increases will come in. The house you have been waiting for is about to be transferred from some man into your possession. The car, the money, and all your stuff is about to be transferred.

Be the *boss* in any recession! Prove to God that He can trust you. When He knows He can flow *through you*, He will flow *to you*. God will provide you with a truckload of seed. Remember, God only provides seed to the sower. Not every Christian gets seed.

When you sow, God multiplies. Most people think God multiplies their seed. That is not actually true. What God multiplies is your resources for sowing. When God is convinced He can trust you, He will continue to supply you with more *resources* for sowing. That means you have more sources established for your increase.

This year it may only be your job. Next year it will be your job and your real estate investments. The year after, you will sow from your job, your real estate investments, and your stock investments. The next year you will sow from all those three plus your businesses. Every year, you will be able to sow more. God will give you ideas about what to invest in. He knows what is going to increase in value. He is always multiplying your resources for sowing.

"Thus you will be enriched in all things and in every way, so that you can be generous, and [your generosity as it is] administered by us will bring forth thanksgiving to God" (2 Corinthians 9:11 AMP).

You are going to be enriched in all things. God will fulfill the desires of your heart. The purpose of all this blessing is so that you can be generous. The Holy Ghost can lead you and fund the Gospel all around the world.

Chapter 13
Isaac Prospered During Famine

Famines were serious business—they make recessions look easy. God's provision during a time of famine was even more significant than His provision during an economic down turn. So let's look at what He did for another servant, Abraham's son, Isaac.

In *Genesis 26:1* it says, *"There was a famine in the land, besides the first famine that was in the days of Abraham. And Isaac went to Abimelech king of the Philistines, in Gerar."* Isaac didn't want to participate in this recession, so he got on his knees and said, "Lord, what is Your instruction?"

> God's provision during a time of famine was even more significant than His provision during an economic down turn.

Here comes the instruction: *"Then the LORD appeared to him and said: 'Do not go down to Egypt'"* (v. 2a). This time, God said He was going to bless him right where he was. He has numbered the hairs on your head, so He knows exactly what you need.

"Live in the land of which I shall tell you" (v. 2b). In other words, God is telling him to do what He tells him to do. Don't do what the

world is doing in a recession. What should you do? Do whatever God tells you to do.

God told him to stay right where he was. Because Isaac prayed and asked God for instruction, God said, "In the middle of this recession, I'm going to bless you." When? In the recession, right where he was. Not only was God going to bless him, He promised, *"I will be with you and bless you; for to you and your descendants I give all these lands"* (v. 3a). When is God going to give all these lands to Isaac? In the recession. And it gets even better. God goes on and says, *"I will perform the oath which I swore to Abraham your father"* (v. 3b).

Look at God's promise to Isaac in verse four: *"And I will make thy seed to multiply as the stars of heaven, and will give unto thy seed all these countries; and in thy seed shall all the nations of the earth be blessed."* When was God going to do this? In the middle of a recession.

Verse five says, *"Because that Abraham obeyed my voice, and kept my charge, my commandments, my statutes, and my laws."* Again, we see that obedience is critical to the blessing.

Did Isaac go down to Egypt, or did he stay in Gerar as God directed him to do? *"And Isaac dwelt in Gerar"* (v. 6).

God said, "If you stay where you are at, I am going to bless you." So the question is this: did God bless Isaac? Read the next two verses; you may experience some déjà vu. *"And the men of the place asked about his wife. And he said, 'She is my sister'; for he was afraid to say, 'She is my wife,' because he thought, 'lest the men of the place kill me for Rebekah, because she is beautiful to behold'"* (Genesis 26:7).

But he didn't receive a blessing right away. You can be in the right place at the right time and yet miss the blessing, because the blessing always follows a seed. Isaac had been there a long time and he had received no blessing.

Verse eight says, *"Now it came to pass, when he had been there a long time, that Abimelech king of the Philistines looked through a window, and saw, and there was Isaac, showing endearment to Rebekah his wife."*

Even though Isaac had been in the right place a long time there was still no blessing. Let's keep reading. The next verse says, *"Then Abimelech called Isaac and said, 'Quite obviously she is your wife; so how could you say, "She is my sister"?' Isaac said to him, 'Because I said, "Lest I die on account of her."'"*

In verse 10 we read, *"And Abimelech said, 'What is this you have done to us? One of the people might soon have lain with your wife, and you would have brought guilt on us.' So Abimelech charged all his people, saying, 'He who touches this man or his wife shall surely be put to death.'"*

There was still no blessing. Why? God said in verse four, *"I will make thy seed to multiply,"* and Isaac had not yet planted seed.

Blessing doesn't follow a need; it follows a seed. That's why God doesn't give you your needs, but He will give you the right seed.

Now look at what happened, *"Then Isaac sowed* [Isaac sowed in the middle of a recession!] *in that land, and received in the same year an hundredfold: and the LORD blessed him"* (v. 12).

> **God doesn't give you your needs, but He will give you the right seed.**

In *Genesis 17* God introduces Himself to Abraham, Isaac's father, in an entirely new way. God said to Abraham, *"To you and your descendants I am Almighty God" (Genesis 17: 1-7).* Before *Genesis 17*, God was known only by two Hebrew names; Jehovah and Elohim. Jehovah means the "Eternal One." Elohim means "the Creator of all natural laws in heaven and on earth." When God said to Abraham, *"I am Almighty God,"* He was using the Hebrew name "El Shaddai."

The name El Shaddai means "more than enough, or all sufficient One." But this is the definition I love best: "I am the One who reserves the right to reverse, overrule, prolong, and accelerate every natural law that Elohim ever created." That's El Shaddai! That's why it didn't take another season for Isaac to receive the hundredfold—he received it in the same year! What did God do? He accelerated the harvest. When did He do that? God did it in the middle of a recession!

> **The speed of your obedience determines the speed of your harvest.**

The speed of your obedience determines the speed of your harvest. Seed can never produce until it hits the ground. Even Isaac did not get a harvest until his seed hit the ground, but when it did, he got the harvest in the same year. El Shaddai can give you a harvest in one day, but He cannot do it if the seed never hits the ground.

Now, watch this. Isaac received the hundredfold, but the hundredfold wasn't actually the blessing. The blessing was about to come. He sowed and he received a hundredfold. Do you know what Isaac did with the hundredfold?

He ate some and sowed the rest, and he got another hundredfold. He ate some, sold the rest, and got another hundredfold. He ate some, sowed the rest, and got another hundredfold.

The Bible, in *The Amplified*, says, *"And the man became great"* in *Genesis 26:13.* That means he became wealthy. He became rich.

And when did this happen? In the middle of a recession—a famine.

Verse thirteen goes on to say, *"And [he] gained more and more until he became very wealthy and distinguished"* (AMP). How rich was he? Look at the next verse. *"He owned flocks, herds, and a great supply of servants"* (AMP).

Isaac had nothing when the recession started except his seed; but because of that seed, he now had flocks. The flocks didn't come from heaven. The Philistines had the flocks, and he was the only one in the recession who had food. So to get some food, they sold their flocks. Isaac ended up with their flocks. Not only that, but he ended up with their herds. These herds didn't come from heaven. They were there all the time. The Philistines had them.

Verse fourteen says he had so much *"the Philistines envied him."* Why were the Philistines envious? Because all their stuff was now in *Isaac's hands* and he became wealthy. Remember in verse one Isaac went to King Abimelech, king of the Philistines, in a famine. Why? Because they had all the stuff—the flocks, herds, servants, and lands. Isaac was broke, and they were rich. Yet by verse sixteen Isaac had become mightier than even King Abimelech. Their wealth had become his wealth!

When did he become rich? In the middle of a recession. Why did Isaac have all of the Philistines' stuff? Because he was the only one who sowed in the middle of a famine, and God blessed him with hundredfold returns.

> **Why does God give seed to the sower? Because the seed contains your harvest!**

Why does God give seed to the sower? Because the seed contains your harvest! Isaac's flocks, herds, and wealth were all hidden in the seed. Had he never sowed, he would never have seen the wealth that God had ready for him. Why? His wealth was hidden in the right seed.

What happens when you give? *Luke 6:38* says: *"Give, and it shall be given unto you; good measure, pressed down, and shaken together, and running over, shall men give into your bosom."*

All this wealth had been waiting for Isaac in the land of the Philistines. The Philistines had those herds and those flocks, and the moment Isaac sowed, they couldn't keep them anymore. All of King Abimelech's wealth was transferred to Isaac.

Any recession can be your harvest season, and you can take acquisition of properties, money, cars, and every form of wealth.

Sowing the Right Measure

Jesus gives a word of warning in the second half of the verse we read above: *"For with the same measure that you use, it will be measured back to you" (Luke 6:38).*

> **The wrong measure of seed can never bring the right measure of harvest.**

You may be asking, "Why do you call that a warning?" **The wrong measure of seed can never bring the right measure of harvest.**

I never got my first harvest in hundreds until I sowed my first hundred-dollar seed. The very night I sowed, someone walked up to me and gave me a check for $360. I was going to Bible school at the time, so that was a whole lot of money. I never got my first harvest in thousands until I sowed my first thousand-dollar seed. Ninety-seven days later, on the night of graduation, someone walked up to me and gave me a check for $16,500.

God is no respecter of persons. He is not trying to bless one and not another, but you are going to have to obey the Word and the voice of the Holy Spirit if you want to walk in His blessing.

We were $35,000 in debt on our building, and God said, "Sow your way out." I sowed a seed in the measure I wanted to receive. Twenty-eight days later, we were totally, completely out of debt. Why? Because my harvest was hidden in my seed, and it wasn't any old seed. It was the seed that God directed me to sow.

Remember, the instruction you obey is the future you create.

> **The instruction you obey is the future you create.**

When God tells us to give a certain amount, are we going to believe there is a breakthrough waiting on the other side of our obedience? If we truly believe, we will sow that seed. Some Christians want to sow just any old seed, but until they sow the right one, their harvest will not come in.

People fear that ministers are just trying to take their money. You should never give what a minister tells you. Only give what God tells you to give. If God says to give it all, you had better obey. God is not interested in your money. Your money cannot help Him in heaven. He is interested in blessing you. The wrong seed can never bring the right harvest.

Chapter 14
Call to Action

Paul's wealth was in Malta. Abraham's wealth was laid up in Egypt. Isaac's wealth was in Gerar where the Philistines lived. Where is your wealth? Every time there was a transfer of wealth in a recession, it did not come from heaven. Wherever God sends you—even if He tells you to stay where you are—wealth and provision await you. Don't miss your place of transfer.

If there ever was a time for the church to walk in all grace, this is the time. We need grace in the middle of a recession. Grace is an earthly blessing. It is not something waiting for you in heaven. God has provided the blessing to you now, here on the earth. Expect every favor and earthly blessing to come upon you during recessions. These blessings are going to come to you in abundance—in the full measure. The purpose of the abundance is so that you will always (even in a recession) have all your needs met and enough left over to contribute to every good work. Grace will put you in a place of abundance.

The key here goes back to something I mentioned earlier—the measure of your giving affects the measure of your blessing. You cannot be stingy and expect overflow in your life. God's level of blessing is contingent upon your measure of seed. Generous givers experience all grace and favor. You will never suffer lack when you give liberally.

In each example we have studied, every blessing that was needed was already located somewhere on the earth. Our blessings are not with God; they are with men. Abraham's blessing was with men in Egypt. Isaac's blessing was with men in Gerar. Joseph's blessing was with men in Canaan and in Egypt. Elijah's blessing was at the brook Cherith. The widow's blessing was with men in Zarephath. The King's blessing was in Edom. The widow's blessing was right there with her neighbors. As you give, God speaks to men to give into your bosom the harvest of that seed.

God cannot just give us our stuff. We have the authority on the earth. What God can do is give us seed. His purpose in giving us seed is so we can make our faith complete. To access our stuff, we need seed. Many faith circles do not understand this critical part of faith.

> **We have to ask God what seed is required for our desired harvest.**

Don't limit God by sowing the wrong measure. **We have to ask God what seed is required for our desired harvest.** He will give a specific amount which will correspond to the level of blessing that you want. When your measure of seed equals your measure of faith, the right harvest will come into your life.

God's heart is to bless you beyond anything you could ever ask or imagine. You tie His hands when your measure of seed does not match your level of faith. He who sows sparingly reaps the same. God has always had a bountiful blessing in mind for you. Your seed today protects your tomorrow. Faith without seed is incomplete, and seed without faith is incomplete.

Experience Blessings Every Day

We can receive an increase of blessings every day. Would you like to begin experiencing this in your life?

Begin by documenting your daily blessings. Buy a journal and write down every good thing that happened that day. All good and perfect gifts come from the Father of lights. Even the small things like getting a great parking spot at the mall should be written down.

Once you write down all the favor you are experiencing, take time to encourage yourself by reading that list of blessings. You will soon realize that you were never in a recession! Blessings are coming upon you and overtaking you. If you want to read anything at all, read your list of blessings! There is always much to be thankful for. Stop looking at what you don't have, and start celebrating what you do have. Thankfulness is the right attitude.

You must put a guard on your mouth. You cannot be releasing the wrong words and then wonder why the right stuff is not coming into your life. You have to speak the right words all the time. You have to believe it before you speak it. You have to speak the "*Word believed.*" When the Word believed is spoken, you are releasing faith. You not only have faith, but you are releasing it through words.

Also, remember that faith without works is dead. Your seed becomes the works of your faith. Seed completes your faith. People are just waiting on a blessing, praying the same prayer over and over. They continue to struggle because they do not understand their faith is incomplete without works. *James 2:17-21* teaches us that it is the seed that completes our faith. Without a seed, there can be no harvest of blessing in our lives.

No Recession for God's Children

God has given a word for today, a word that we, His children, are not supposed to listen to the voices of doubt and fear around us but to His voice. He has a plan for you—an ark of safety, a brook running with water in the middle of drought and famine.

But as we have seen from examples in His Word, we must indeed discipline ourselves. We must follow the steps He has laid out and use the keys to blessing He's provided. He has provided His Word for us to believe, His Holy Spirit to guide us, and He meets our needs as we sow our seed.

God has desired to bless us from the beginning—since Adam and Eve in the Garden. Yet mankind took a path of disobedience, and the Kingdom of God on earth didn't start in the Garden as God intended. The devil has been trying to keep us in disobedience ever since.

God wants to bless us, for He is coming soon, and we must use that blessing to, in turn, spread His Kingdom power and anointing onto those who need it. Paul understood that—that obedience would bring the blessing while disobedience would prevent it. Therefore, when he arrived in Rome, after blessing an entire island despite the shipwreck and snakebite, he came blessed and fully loaded.

It's time for us to take our authority as believers—the authority that Jesus Christ received from His Father and gave unto us, God's children. It's time for us to stop whining when the devil tries to load our circumstances up and prevent us from using God's keys to blessings. It's time for us to take our authority, for our God is greater than the god of this world!

It may be a time of famine, but that only means it's planting time in God's Kingdom!

It may be a time of famine, but that only means it's planting time in God's Kingdom!

Staying in faith and obedience is the most important thing you can do right now. Weapons will be formed against you, but He has given you the authority to decide if they prosper.

If you have not obeyed, if you have not followed God's prescribed way of blessing you, it's time for one thing—repent! Turn from your sin, ask Him forgiveness, and *get back on top!*

No more "tipping" God. No more leftovers or blemished, unworthy sacrifices. It's time for us to shake off the serpent of doubt and fear that's trying to kill us and stay grounded in our God, El Shaddai!

In **Genesis 26**, Isaac sowed during a famine; he obeyed the instruction and prospered. The Scriptures tell us that he received herds, flocks, and lands from all around him! As you sow, I believe that God will cause the wealth of the world around you to start coming *your* way.

As we read, all the provision and wealth was already there—in the hands of men waiting to be transferred to God's people during a recession. That's the way it is now. Your provision and wealth are also here waiting on your seed.

> **Your provision and wealth are here waiting on your seed.**

Now is the time to be the *boss* over this recession and over your circumstances. Be a doer of the Word.

A. **B**elieve the Word.

B. **O**bey God's instruction.

C. **S**ow the right **S**eed.

If you have been blessed with this teaching, then obey God. **Galatians 6:6** says, *"Let him who is taught the word share in all good things with him who teaches."* As you follow the seven steps below, you will see prosperity in the middle of any recession.

Seven Steps to Your Harvest

There are seven steps to receive your harvest:

1. Give your seed an assignment; focus your faith on what you are releasing your seed for. (There is a Recession Breakthrough Seed form on page 141 for you to fill out. Make sure you write down what you are believing God for.)

2. Pray. Ask God what measure of seed to give or follow the principle of *Luke 6:38,* which says, *"Give, and it will be given to you: good measure, pressed down, shaken together, and running over will be put into your bosom. For with the same measure that you use, it will be measured back to you."* Sow in the measure you want to receive.

3. Obey God's instruction. Your blessing is waiting on the other side of your obedience to sow.

4. Never let your seed travel alone. The seed needs nutrients to grow. Faith is that nutrient. You release faith with your words. The Bible says to believe you receive when you pray *(Mark 11:24)*. Say, *"I receive…"* as you sow your seed.

5. Send in your prayer request and seed and we will pray the prayer of agreement and release our faith for your harvest and blessing. *Matthew 18:19* says, *"Again I say to you that if two of you agree on earth concerning anything that they ask, it will be done for them by My Father in heaven."*

6. Now enter God's rest. Don't worry; don't ask again. Just thank Him that it's already released and on its way. The more you thank Him, the faster it manifests.

7. As you **believe** His Word, **o**bey His instruction, and **s**ow the right seed, not only will you not be touched by any recession but you will prosper because you are in the place of transfer.

So, my friend, I leave you with this; will you choose to participate in recessions, or will you choose to participate in times of blessing? These are our greatest opportunities for wealth transfer—become the *BOSS* of any recession!

I pray you choose to receive an extravagant harvest!

I'll see you at the top.

About the Author

Dr. Nasir K. Siddiki is a nationally acclaimed minister, speaker, and business leader who is well-known for teaching on biblical principles of success and financial increase. During his more than twenty-five years of combined marketing and management experience, Dr. Siddiki directed several new companies to multi-million dollar success stories.

Even more extraordinary was the miracle he experienced after being diagnosed with the worst case of shingles ever admitted to Toronto General Hospital. At the age of 34, born into a Muslim family, the doctors had given up on him. They had determined that his immune system had shut down; with 107.6 degree temperature, his body had stopped fighting. Aware of their conversation and having put all his trust in the doctors he cried out, "God, if you're real, don't let me die!" That night in his darkest hour, Jesus appeared at his bedside and said, "I Am the God of the Christians. I Am the God of Abraham, Isaac and Jacob." That brief moment in Jesus' presence left Nasir Siddiki miraculously healed. Since then Dr. Siddiki's passion has been to know and serve the Lord Jesus Christ.

Currently he teaches scriptural success principles to businessmen and churches throughout the U.S. and internationally. He hosts the television program "Winning With Wisdom" seen all over the world on TBN and other television networks.

Dr. Siddiki presently lives with his wife, Anita, and their two children in Tulsa, Oklahoma, where Wisdom Ministries is based.

"Take Your Finances to the Next Level"

Kingdom Principles
of
FINANCIAL INCREASE

You don't have to live in financial bondage any longer! God has provided everything you need to live in His abundance. Now your prosperity lies in your hands as you follow His Kingdom principles for financial increase.

In this book, Dr. Nasir Siddiki teaches you biblical principles to lead you straight out of poverty and lack into God's abundant life of prosperity and financial success.

In *Kingdom Principles of Financial Increase*, Dr. Nasir Siddiki presents one of the most profound, yet simple, approaches to this essential subject. His logical, yet deeply spiritual presentation of these biblical principles for financial management, giving and receiving, provide a balanced view of a much misunderstood topic.

Dr. Myles Munroe

To order your copy visit our Online Store at
www.wisdomministries.org

Free Magazine Offer

Miracles Today!

Visit our website and order your free copy today!

The Miracles Today magazine is filled with dynamic miracle testimonies about Dr. Nasir Siddiki and his family.

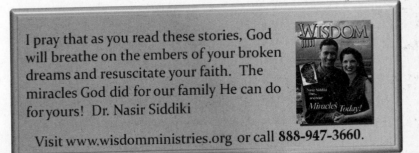

You're Invited! Each month people come from all over the country to hear Dr. Siddiki live at the Wisdom Center in Tulsa, Oklahoma. If you are interested in attending one of these life-changing events, you can find out more information by clicking on the "Meeting Information" button at www.wisdomministries.org.

"Teaching of the Word and Impartations at the Wisdom Center, Tulsa, Oklahoma"

Live Streaming of all Conferences

Visit www.wisdomministries.org and click on the "Live Streaming " button to register and to find out when the next live event is scheduled. Click on "Video On Demand" button and watch archived "Winning With Wisdom" TV programs and past Wisdom Conferences.

FREE
Teaching Downloads by Dr. Nasir Siddiki

Wisdom Ministries is now offering a fresh, relevant teaching from Dr. Siddiki every week!

Be inspired! Be refreshed! Receive the knowledge you need to be an overcomer in the Kingdom of God!

It is the glory of God to conceal a matter, but the glory of kings is to search out a matter (Prov. 25:2). The treasures of God's Word are not lying on the surface, easily taken by any by passer. You must dig deep to find them. Let Dr. Siddiki help you to dig deep and uncover treasures from God's Word.

**SIGN UP TODAY AT OUR WEBSITE FOR
"FREE TEACHING DOWNLOADS"
FROM DR. NASIR SIDDIKI!
(Teaching lessons are in PDF file format)**

www.wisdomministries.org

Are you looking to further your knowledge of the Word of God? Consider Wisdom University Online.

Earn your degree—pursue your dreams!

Wisdom University is dedicated to reaching people and equipping God's leaders with wisdom from the uncompromised Word of God.

You can earn an Associate, Bachelor, Master, and Doctorate Degree online, affordably, and at your convenience. Turn your passion for God's Word into a degree.

Wisdom University will also honor existing credits from other colleges and universities and, where applicable, bestow on you credits for experience.

Welcome

Anita and I welcome you to the Wisdom University Online. We are dedicated to reaching people and equipping God's leaders with Wisdom.

Dr. Nasir and Anita Siddiki

You have always wanted it, now you can do it online!

See our website for more information and register today!

Accreditation through Transworld Accrediting Commission International, Riverside, California.

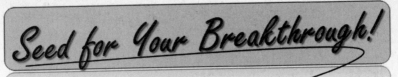

Seed for Your Breakthrough!

"God is able to make it up to you by giving you everything you need and more, so that there will not only be enough for your own needs, but plenty left over to give joyfully to others." (2 Corinthians 9:8)

When you sow your Recession Breakthrough Seed, this becomes the corresponding action that completes your faith (James 2:22). The Bible says that when two agree on earth as touching anything (your seed) it will be done by our Father in heaven. We will pray the prayer of agreement for your financial breakthrough and release our faith over your seed for the corresponding harvest.

You can send your seed through our website at www.wisdomministries.org. Click on the "Online Giving" button. Or, you may use this form and mail it to: Wisdom Ministries – 2748 E. 15th Street, Tulsa, OK 74104

Please write what you are believing God for... _____
_____
_____
_____

Name:					Date:
Address:					
City:					State:
Country:			Zip/Postal Code:		
Home Phone:			Cell Phone:		
Email Address:					
Cash	Check #:	Visa	Master Card	Amer. Ex.	Discover
Credit Card #:					
Exp. Date:			Total Enclosed:		
Signature:					

WISDOM
MINISTRIES

Prayer Requests &
Praise Reports

"Again I say to you that if two of you agree on earth
concerning anything that they ask, it will be done for
them by My Father in heaven." (Matthew 18:19)

We would consider it an honor to pray for you. Send us your
prayer requests and share with us what you are believing God
for. Also, send us your Praise Reports. We love to hear how God
has blessed you through this ministry. Send them to: Wisdom
Ministries—PO Box 4700—Tulsa, OK 74159, or call 918-712-7122.

_____

_____

_____

_____

_____

_____

_____

_____

_____

_____

_____

_____

_____

Become A Partner With Dr. Nasir Siddiki & Wisdom Ministries

Covenant Partners are people, churches and businesses that give to our ministry on a regular basis. We also consider those who give generous one-time gifts of support to be Partners in our vision to reach the lost. As a blessing to those who help us to evangelize the world for Jesus, we offer many Partner Benefits.

Partnership Has Benefits:

More Personal Ministry Each month Covenant Partners receive a special Partner Letter straight from the desk of Dr. Nasir Siddiki. It is ministry by mail filled with exactly what God is putting on Dr. Siddiki's heart each month.

More Personal Prayer We believe in the power of prayer and pray for our Partners every day, whether they send in a prayer request or not. Partners are the backbone of our evangelistic work; we pray for them every day!

More Teaching Partners have access to more teaching from the heart of Dr. Nasir Siddiki than anyone else! With your partnership you will receive discounted rates on items purchased from the media library when you call **918-712-7122**, **9**am - **5**pm (CST).

More Importantly - Heavenly Rewards The greatest benefit is simply knowing that people's lives are being changed. People are being saved, healed, and set free because of your prayers and faithful financial support.

Your support does so much. Pray about becoming a Covenant Partner with our ministry. No gift is too small or too large. Every gift helps us to reach people and change lives for Christ.

To become a Covenant Partner, you make the simple commitment to:

- Pray regularly for Dr. Siddiki and Wisdom Ministries.
- Support the efforts of Wisdom Ministries regularly as God directs your monthly giving.

If you are interested in being a part of our vision and want to become a Covenant Partner, visit our website at www.wisdomministries.org and click on the "Partnership" button, or call **918-712-7122**, **9**am - **5**pm (CST).

Partner Testimonies

Your teaching on reaping and sowing has totally changed my approach to life. I ... sowed $14. Being on disability from my job, I was concerned about paying my rent. That same week...I received a check from my job for $243. I immediately re-sowed $31 into ministries. The next week I received a check for $472. Now that my rent is paid, I can't wait to sow more seed toward your ministry. **C. W., Ohio**

Praise God! I planted a seed of $5 into this ministry which was my last $5 at the time. I was believing for 100 fold on seed sown. I was blessed with an unexpected check for $500 in 3 days after planting seed. **Carol, Oklahoma**

I sowed a $1,000 seed believing God to meet my needs. I was then blessed with a sales job earning salary, commissions and benefits. I once again sowed another $1,000 seed. Shortly after I was offered a better job with a $25,000 a year increase in salary, plus commissions and great benefits. Praise God! **Sheri, Oklahoma**

In March, we used our tax return and planted a $2000 seed to be debt free. In August, we received 60 fold return, an inheritance of $123,000. We were able to pay off most of our debt, with the exception of some of our mortgage. **Ron & Karen, Oregon**

Many, many thanks for your teaching on TBN that saved my life. I nearly committed suicide when my heart told me to tune to your program...I had a lot of debt to pay and had no other way in my own understanding but to die. But thank God that you spoke in my life and I gave my life to Christ the same day. **L.K., Zambia**

Thank you for the tremendous deposit that you left at our church. Our ministry will never be the same after having received the impartation and the anointing from your ministry. Many positive things have taken place in our ministry...Our general offerings have increased and held steady by 30%...Our instruction times have been taken to another dimension. I have highly recommended you and your ministry to churches across the nation. **Pastor Lonnie, Michigan**

I was at a seminar with Dr. Siddiki and all I can say is wow! The teaching was incredible, but when it came time to make an offering I started getting really uncomfortable. I prayed about it and an amount was placed on my heart. I said, "Lord, I can't afford that much, that's a bill that needs to be paid." I wrote my check and the whole time I'm saying to myself, "You can't do this." I ended up leaving that service with my check still in hand. All day it weighed on my heart and mind. I am a tither and I have sown and seen results, but I just kept telling myself, "You can't give that much right now." When I came back for the evening service, I placed that envelope in the offering bucket and said, "Okay Lord, it's in your hands." The next morning, I was at work about 10 minutes when I was offered a promotion that will increase my salary by $5000-$10,000 a year. Praise God! **Teri, New York**

Watch Dr. Siddiki on "Winning With Wisdom" TV Broadcast

Trinity Broadcasting Network and other TV networks

Check our website for times and locations

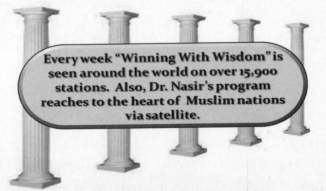

Every week "Winning With Wisdom" is seen around the world on over 15,900 stations. Also, Dr. Nasir's program reaches to the heart of Muslim nations via satellite.

www.wisdomministries.org

WISDOM MINISTRIES
Vision5000

Join Vision 5000 and learn how to invest in the stock market led by the Holy Spirit!

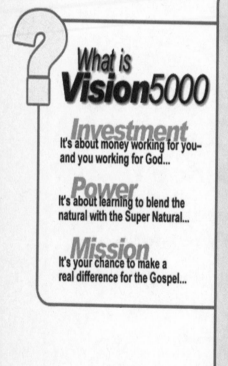

What is Vision5000

Investment
It's about money working for you–
and you working for God...

Power
It's about learning to blend the
natural with the Super Natural...

Mission
It's your chance to make a
real difference for the Gospel...

God has instructed me to train up 5000 people so that they will have both the knowledge they need to be successful in the area of the stock market, as well as the ability to clearly hear the voice of God. Armed with this knowledge, these 5000 will be in a position to fund the last great harvest.

For those that are serious about becoming a financial distribution center for God, through which He will fund His end time harvest, Vision5000 is a great place to start.

If you feel that God is leading you in this area, then join our Vision 5000 team. By becoming a member it will allow us to help train you and give you the support you need to fulfill God's plan for your life.

Dr. Nasir Siddiki

To join or find out more information log on to www.wisdomministries.org and click on the "Vision5000" button.

Product Catalog

Teaching by Dr. Nasir Siddiki

Take your faith and relationship with
God to the next level or give a gift
that will change a life forever.

	FINANCES	6 CDs	QTY	TOTAL
CVD001	How to Prosper in Any Recession (3 CDs/3 DVDs)	$30		
CDS035	Life After Debt	$30		
CDS021	Harness the Power of Money	$30		
CDS031	Kingdom Principles of Financial Increase	$30		
CDS024	How to Access All Things	$30		
CDS036	Managing Money God's Way	$30		
CDS043	Offerings that God Must Multiply	$30		
CDS046	Prosperity - Motives of the Heart	$30		
CDS062	What Feeds the Seed	$30		
CDS073	The Harvest Twins - Faith & Seed 1	$30		
CDS074	The Harvest Twins - Faith & Seed 2	$30		
CDS015	Favor with God and Man	$30		
CDS077	The Favor Connection 1	$30		
CDS083	The Favor Connection 2	$30		
CDS019	God's Prerequisite for Wealth	$30		
	HEALING			
CDS086	The Healing Twins-Faith and Anointing	$30		
CDS022	Healing Made Simple	$30		
CDS028	How to Keep Your Healing	$30		
CDS030	Issues that Stop Your Healing	$30		
CDS042	Obtaining Your Healing - Anita & Dr. Siddiki	$30		
	PRAYER			
CDS089	Answers to Your 10 Most Frequent Prayers	$30		
CDS087	Prayer That Releases Power	$30		
CDS045	Prayer Currency of the Kingdom	$30		
CDS044	Prayer that Moves Angels	$30		
CDS049	Secrets of Successful Prayer	$30		
CDS075	When Prayer is Not Enough 1	$30		
CDS076	When Prayer is Not Enough 2	$30		
CDS018	The Character of God	$30		
	BUSINESS			
CDS065	Wisdom for Business 1	$30		
CDS066	Wisdom for Business 2	$30		
CDS037	Flying High in Business 1	$30		
CDS016	Flying High in Business 2	$30		

		SPIRIT LED INVESTING	6 CDs	QTY	TOTAL
	CDS063	Winning on Wall Street 1	$30		
	CDS064	Winning on Wall Street 2	$30		
	CDS009	Common Sense Trading Led by the Holy Spirit	$30		
	CDS059	Vision 5000 Training 1	$30		
	CDS060	Vision 5000 Training 2	$30		
	CDS061	Vision 5000 Training 3	$30		
		BLESSING			
	CDS090	Released to Reign	$30		
	CDS085	Your Seat of Power	$30		
	CDS084	The Blessing that Maketh Rich	$30		
	CDS079	How the Blessings Flow	$30		
	CDS080	Obedience - Key to the Blessing	$30		
	CDS081	Faith is the Blessing Connection	$30		
	CDS082	Pray & Obey	$30		
	CDS078	Living in the Blessing	$30		
	CDS047	How to Receive Your Commanded Blessing	$30		
		FAITH			
	CDS091	The Laws of Confession	$30		
	CDS013	Faith that Brings Victory	$30		
	CDS014	Faith that Cannot Fail	$30		
	CDS048	The Rest of Faith	$30		
		HOW THE ENEMY ATTACKS			
	CDS088	Your Mind-The Final Battleground	$30		
	CDS050	Strongholds 1—Free From Fear	$30		
	CDS051	Strongholds 2—How the Enemy Attacks	$30		
	CDS052	Strongholds 3—The Law of Thought & Harvest	$30		
	CDS053	Strongholds 4—Enter & Live in His Rest	$30		
	CDS054	Strongholds 5—The Armor	$30		
	CDS055	Strongholds 6—Releasing the Fruit of the Spirit	$30		
	CDS056	Strongholds 7—Devil Knows Your Hot Button	$30		
		SPIRITUAL GROWTH			
	CDS001	Authority of the Believer 1	$30		
	CDS002	Authority of the Believer 2	$30		
	CDS003	Becoming A Spiritual Giant 1	$30		
	CDS004	Becoming A Spiritual Giant 2	$30		
	CDS020	Growing Up Spiritually	$30		
	CDS025	How to Increase the Anointing 1	$30		
	CDS026	How to Increase the Anointing 2	$30		
	CDS027	How to Increase the Anointing 3	$30		

		SPIRITUAL GROWTH	6 CDs	QTY	TOTAL
CDS005		Bridge to the Spiritual Realm - Anita & Dr Siddiki	$30		
CDS012		Explosive Power of God's Word	$30		
		LEADERSHIP			
CDS034		Leadership Principles 1—Taking Jesus to the Marketplace	$30		
CDS032		Leadership Principles 2—Accomplishing Vision	$30		
CDS033		Leadership Principles 3—Discipline-Key to Learning God's Voice	$30		
CDS072		Mark Of A Winner	$30		
CDS006		Catching the Spirit of Excellence 1	$30		
CDS007		Catching the Spirit of Excellence 2	$30		
CDS008		Catching the Spirit of Excellence 3	$30		
		MARRIAGE & FAMILY			
CDS067		Wisdom for Successful Living	$30		
CDS040		Marriage 1—God's Plan - Heaven on Earth	$30		
CDS041		Marriage 2—Sizzling Sex - God's Way	$30		
CDS038		Marriage 3—Communication is the Key	$30		
CDS039		Marriage 4—Differences Between Men & Women	$30		
CDS071		Marriage 5—His Needs - Her Needs	$30		
CDS017		For Men Only	$30		
		THE VOICE OF GOD			
CDS029		How to Know the Voice of God	$30		
CDS023		Hearing the Voice of the Holy Spirit - Anita Siddiki	$30		
CDS058		Right Decisions - The Key to Your Success	$30		
CDS057		The Person of the Holy Spirit	$30		
		WORSHIP			
CDS068		Worship 1—Drawing Near to God	$30		
CDS069		Worship 2—Drawing Near to God	$30		
CDS070		Worship 3—Entering the Holy of Holies	$30		
CDS010		Experiencing God's Glory 1	$30		
CDS011		Experiencing God's Glory 2	$30		
		DVD			
DVD001		How to Receive Your Miracle (1 DVD)	$10		
DVD002		Praying out the Blessing (3 DVD)	$30		
DVD003		The Extravagant Blessing (3 DVD)	$30		
DVD004		Driving Debt Out of Your Life (3 DVD)	$30		
CVD001		How to Prosper in Any Recession (3 CDs/3 DVDs)	$30		
		BOOKS & MANUALS			
BK001		Kingdom Principles of Financial Increase - Book	$12.95		
MN001		Common Sense Trading Led by the Holy Spirit-MN	$20		
MN002		Winning on Wall Street - MN	$20		
		SUBTOTAL	$		

WISDOM MINISTRIES

Product Ordering Form

Postage and Handling

Purchase Amount	US	Foreign
0 - $ 29.99	$4	$ 7.95
$ 30 - $ 49.99	$5	$11.95
$ 50 - $ 74.99	$6	$13.95
$ 75 - $ 99.99	$7	$15.95
$100 - $124.99	$8	$17.95
$125 - $149.99	$9	$19.95
$150 +	10%	20%

Int'l USPS – 20% of order + U.S. ship cost

SUBTOTAL	
Shipping	
Offering	
Total	

Payment & Shipping Information (Please Print)

Name:	Date:
Shipping Address:	
City:	State:
Country:	Zip/Postal Code:
Home Phone:	Cell Phone:
Email Address:	

Cash	Check #:	Visa	Master Card	Amer. Ex	Discover

Credit Card #:	
Exp. Date:	Total Enclosed:
Signature:	

Please send this order form to: Wisdom Ministries
PO Box 4700 Tulsa, OK 74159
918-712-7122
To order online go to www.wisdomministries.org

Salvation Prayer

If you've never received Jesus Christ as your Savior and Lord, you can do it today. He is waiting to come into your heart and give you eternal life and a better life here and now. Pray this simple prayer from your heart and your life will be forever changed:

"Dear God, I come before You and I admit that I'm a sinner, and I ask your forgiveness. I thank You for sending Jesus to the cross to pay the penalty for my sin. I believe in my heart and confess with my mouth that Jesus is my Lord. I believe that He died on the cross, rose again and now sits at Your right hand. I receive Jesus now as my Lord and Savior. Thank you for coming into my heart and changing me. I will serve You for the rest of my life. I pray this in the precious name of Jesus. Amen."

Call, write or email us if you prayed this prayer for the first time. We would like to send you materials to help you live a victorious life.

Call: **918-712-7122**, or **888-947-3660**
Write: Wisdom Ministries-PO Box 4700-Tulsa, OK 74159
Email: drnsiddiki@wisdomministries.org